BEECHING

BEECHING

50 Years On

ANTHONY POULTON-SMITH

First published 2013

The History Press
The Mill, Brimscombe Port
Stroud, Gloucestershire, GL5 2QG
www.thehistorypress.co.uk

British Library Cataloguing in Publication Data.
A catalogue record for this book is available from the British Library.

ISBN 978 0 7524 8092 3

Typesetting and origination by The History Press
Printed in Great Britain

CONTENTS

INTRODUCTION

March 2013 marks fifty years since the Beeching Axe fell upon the nation's railway system. The recommendations made by the infamous report were greeted with horror and indignation then and the furore is rekindled simply at the mention of Beeching's name.

Dr Richard Beeching was a businessman; he had no connection with the railways. Thus any decisions that were made were based solely upon the logic of profit margins, efficiency and reinvestment, never to be swayed by sentiment. Yet still his name is remembered in an almost Quisling-esque light as the man who decimated the railways. Even British situation comedy used his infamy: thirty years after its publication, writers David Croft and Richard Spendlove, in conjunction with the BBC, produced twenty episodes in a series entitled *Oh, Doctor Beeching!*

Five decades have passed and, with hindsight, we now see that the report did more than any other factor to preserve the nation's railway heritage. Without it the buildings, disused lines, locomotives, rolling stock, signalling systems and signs would simply have been removed and tucked into a corner to be forgotten, or even rotted away.

In this book we shall look at the positive effects the report has had, not on the railways themselves – that has been done many times – but on the opportunities which would never have arisen otherwise. We shall look at the gentle gradients of old lines, perfect for walkers and cyclists alike. Buildings, no longer used as stations and sheds, are now private residences, small businesses, holiday homes and public meeting places. Memorabilia, often described as railwayana, which would otherwise have rusted away, now command prices at collectors' auctions which would astound those who lovingly painted and polished them.

And, of course, we shall look at the heritage railways which attract many thousands each year. They not only allow volunteers to enjoy railways at a level they could otherwise never have imagined, they have also provided employment for others as engineers, station staff, and so on.

Maybe by the end of the book Dr Beeching will be seen in a slightly different light by the reader: not as the saviour of Britain's railways, but as someone whose name should be associated with a whole new area of leisure for all and indeed pleasure for those who can swap OO gauge for 4ft 8in (1.44m).

I   THE INFAMOUS REPORT

27 March 1963 saw the release of one of the most infamous documents in living memory. It ranks alongside Neville Chamberlain's return to Britain when he waved a small piece of paper and proudly proclaimed 'Peace for our time!' exactly eleven months before he declared war.

Three years after the prime minister announced that the government intended to ensure profitability for the railways once again, the report's recommendations were published. It cited a number of apparently appalling statistics. For example, out of 4,300 stations in Britain, more than half realised annual receipts of £10,000, with around 1,700 of these generating under £2,500 per annum. This meant the most profitable 2,000 stations were producing 98 per cent of the income from passenger services. Looking at it another way, a third of the rail miles failed to produce even 1 per cent of the income.

The report used these figures, with specific examples, to demand the closure of 6,000 miles of branch lines (a third of the total length of the railways in the entire country) and 2,363 stations (more than half the nation's total). It also targeted freight services, pointing out that the new container wagons were perfect for carrying coal and ores; the old closed wagons were to be avoided as they were inefficient.

The report also recommended the electrification of some lines but did not dwell on the end of steam, as this had already been decided by British Rail (BR) some years before. It did, however, touch upon the improvement of working terms and conditions for British Rail staff, although specifics were noticeable by their absence.

What is rarely realised is there were actually two reports. Released two years later, the second concentrated on investment and the establishment of 3,000 miles of major trunk routes running between the cities in the four corners of England. North of the border only Glasgow, Edinburgh and Aberdeen were serviced, and forget any part of Wales away from the southern coastline as far as Swansea. That this second report is rarely mentioned is solely down to it being rejected by the government. Note this was now a government under Harold Wilson's leadership, the Labour party having ousted the Conservatives shortly after the original report was published. Whether this decision was political or not will never be known, especially not five decades later.

Even in 1965 there was a difference of opinion between the two main individuals. While Frank Cousins (Minister of Technology) revealed later in the year that Richard Beeching had been sacked by Tom Fraser (Minister of Transport), the latter never confirmed or denied this. Furthermore, Beeching, who had returned to ICI in November 1965, emphatically denied he was sacked but insisted the remaining length of his five-year contract simply did not give him sufficient time to produce a third report. Although never stated so publicly, Richard Beeching never hid that the appointment was temporary and his secondment from ICI was limited to five years. It seems likely neither Beeching nor ICI would have allowed any delay in his return to ICI.

Fifty years on it is no good looking at the report to see what closed, only what was recommended for closure. It should also be noted that some of the closed lines effectively isolated other lines which were considered profitable and were to remain open. However, without connecting trains commuting became impossible and these lines invariably followed their neighbours. Whether or not this was a deliberate policy is impossible to know for certain. Although Beeching was an efficient individual, the sheer size of the task at hand, including having to track passengers as they switched from one line to another, could easily have affected the accuracy of his final figures. A passenger purchases his or her return ticket on one line in the morning, changes to a second and even a third line, and later takes the identical journey but in reverse. The purchase of the ticket would be recorded at the point of departure and even the return, but was any of that fare allocated to any other line as no fare had been paid directly to it?

2   THE MAN HIMSELF

Dr Richard Beeching was born on the Isle of Sheppey on 21 April 1913. The second of four brothers, his father was a reporter with the *Kent Messenger* and his mother a schoolteacher. Soon after his birth he moved to Maidstone, where he was educated at the local Church of England primary school, winning scholarships enabling him to attend Maidstone Grammar School. Thereafter he went on to the Imperial College of Science and Technology in London, taking first-class honours degrees in physics. He stayed on to complete his Ph.D., working at the Fuel Research Station in Greenwich and at the Mond Nickel Laboratories, where he was appointed senior physicist in the research of physics, metallurgy and mechanical engineering. In 1938 he married Ella Tiley, whom he

had known since his schooldays in Maidstone. Their forty-six-year marriage did
not produce any children.

With the outbreak of the Second World War, Beeching was recommended
as the ideal man to work in Armament Design and Research, with a rank
equivalent to that of army captain, where he worked under Sir Frank Smith.
The two men were reunited at ICI in 1948, working on products as diverse as
paints, zip fasteners and leathers, looking to reduce production costs and improve
efficiency. He stayed with ICI in a number of roles for nine years, including two
years in Canada, returning to Britain where he was appointed chairman of ICI
Metals Division.

In 1961 Ernest Marples of the British Transport Commission, a body chaired by
Sir Ivan Stedeford (hence the group being referred to as the Stedeford Committee),
invited Sir Frank Smith to join them by heading an advisory group. Smith had
retired two years earlier and suggested they approach Beeching instead, which
resulted in the publication of the Beeching Report and, ultimately, this book.

Less well documented are the continual clashes between Stedeford and
Beeching, with the former disagreeing with the drastic cuts planned in the
report. Stedeford opposed most of the reduction in the length of the track and
fervently believed scrapping over 300,000 freight wagons would effectively force
everything on to the road.

Beeching was appointed chairman of the British Railways Board from June
1961. The announcement made front-page headlines, not so much for the
appointment as for the annual salary of £24,000. To put this extraordinary amount
into perspective, it was £14,000 more than Prime Minister Harold Macmillan
earned and £15,000 more than any other leader of a nationalised concern. It was
based on his salary at ICI and in his defence he did not set the rate himself, other
than perhaps to ask for the same as he was already receiving – and most would be
expected to do the same in that position.

It did, however, serve to put him in a bad light with the public, most of whom
would never otherwise have known of his existence; suddenly he was pocketing
huge amounts of taxpayers' money. Taxation took its toll on Beeching, too; rates
of the day meant he was receiving no more than £7,000 – but the old adage of
'one must be earning it to pay it' gave him no respite.

He was not benefiting financially from the deal; his employers ICI had made it
clear they wanted him back and this was a leave of absence of no more than five
years. Compare his salary against the £42 million British Rail had lost in 1960
and, should he prove to be the right man for the job, this would clearly be money
well spent.

Already a controversial figure because of his salary, the release of *The Reshaping
of British Railways* on 27 March 1963 probably made Richard Beeching the most
unpopular man in the country since Jack the Ripper. Instantly mistrusted by those
members of the public still using the railways regularly, the opposition Labour

party targeted him at every opportunity, while the huge weight of opinion of the trade unions was unsurprisingly against the recommendations.

In February 1965 the second stage of the upheaval was announced: not additional cuts, but where future investment and reshaping would further streamline the organisation and increase efficiency and profitability. This came only two months after it was announced that Beeching would be returning to ICI in November 1965, just four years after his appointment. By now the nation had a Labour government under Harold Wilson, although perhaps this was not relevant in the rejection of the second part of Beeching's plan.

Returning to his previous employer, he was made Baron Beeching of East Grinstead in the Queen's birthday honours list of 1965, ICI making him deputy chairman the following year. He continued in a series of roles until his retirement in 1977. Richard Beeching died on 23 March 1985 at Queen Victoria Hospital, East Grinstead, West Sussex, twenty-nine days short of his seventy-second birthday.

3   WEST SOMERSET RAILWAY

Today one of the country's railway arteries links Bristol and Exeter, as it has since the earliest days of the railways, two of the most important cities in the West Country. Travelling by sea meant rounding the Cornish coastline and the very real dangers associated with that rocky route. Thus an alternative was sought to avoid the delays in the busy port of Bristol and provide a link between the Severn Estuary and the English Channel on the south coast. Several routes were suggested, unsurprisingly each hoped to promote the local port and attract business to the harbours of Watchet, Porlock, or Minehead in Somerset, while others covered almost all the northern coastline of Somerset, Devon and part of Cornwall.

More than ten years after discussions began and still not one had become anything more than an idea. In July 1856 a meeting was held to discuss linking the Bristol & Exeter Railway at Taunton or Bridgwater with Watchet. Linked with the West Somerset Mineral Railway, then under construction, this would bring coal from the South Wales fields to Somerset at a fraction of the current cost.

With a number of problems arising, a second meeting was called three weeks later when Isambard Kingdom Brunel could attend and offer his invaluable input to finding a solution. Never one to avoid the difficult, or apparently impossible, and always keen to flaunt his engineering genius, Brunel spoke of a long tunnel beneath the Quantocks and pushing the line back as far as Minehead or Porlock. He failed and it was decided to link Watchet to Taunton.

So a year later, on 17 August 1857, the required Act of Parliament was passed, the West Somerset Railway Company formed, and the steps to raise the £120,000 required were well under way. Incidentally, the target figure was reached before the end of the year – roughly £1,000 a day, something the modern West Somerset Railway would certainly welcome and a great achievement in early Victorian Britain.

Construction began, under the engineer George Furness, in April 1859 and the first passenger train ran from Watchet to Taunton almost three years later to the day, with goods traffic following in August that year. Initially these trains came through to Taunton Station as no separate junction was provided until 1871, when it was linked to the Devon & Somerset Railway and the station built at Norton Fitzwarren. Early plans to link with the West Somerset Mineral Railway never materialised; despite much protest this line never reached Watchet. However, the West Somerset Railway, after a couple of false starts, was extended as far as Minehead.

Thus, in 1874 almost 23 miles of single track were built, with a passing loop at the approximate midway point of Williton. By 1876, and now amalgamated with the Great Western Railway (GWR) but still an independent company, a second loop opened at Crowcombe Heathfield. In an amazing feat of engineering efficiency, 1882 saw the conversion of the GWR broad gauge (7ft ¼in) to standard gauge (4ft 8½in). Trains ran as normal on Saturday 28 October 1882, but Sunday saw the track lifted and replaced, with trains running again on Monday afternoon.

The capacity of the GWR enabled the platform at Stogumber to be extended in 1900, a passing loop installed at Blue Anchor four years later, and a second platform introduced at Minehead in 1905. In 1907 a loop was incorporated into the Bishops Lydeard station, with the original at Williton extended the same year to allow longer trains to pass.

The Railways Act of 1921 saw the West Somerset Railway finally become fully amalgamated with the GWR, only to change again with nationalisation on the stroke of midnight on 31 December 1947. By then, further improvements had

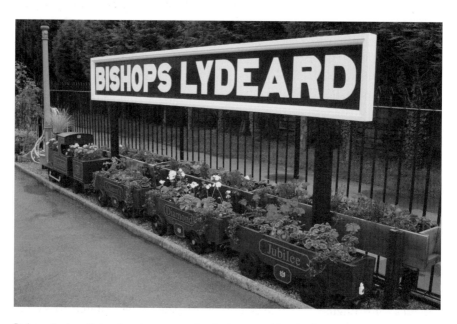

Bishops Lydeard's station sign appropriately decorated for the Diamond Jubilee of Queen Elizabeth II. (*Author*)

been made with a longer loop at Blue Anchor, and double track laid between Dunster and Minehead, and from Norton Fitzwarren to Bishops Lydeard.

In the five years leading up to the Second World War, so-called 'camp coaches' were parked at Blue Anchor and Stogumber. These provided accommodation for holidaymakers who were hopefully attracted to the new open-air swimming pool at Minehead, built at a cost of £20,000 by GWR. For those travelling by train to the destination, a package deal was offered, with the cost of accommodation included in the train ticket.

These camp coaches reappeared in 1952 and served the public until 1964. However, the opening of the Butlins camp in 1962 proved more of an attraction and 30,000 people booked into the holiday camp in the first year alone. Thus, from 1964 to 1970 the camp coaches were used solely for British Rail staff and their families as a holiday base.

Not even Butlins could prevent the line appearing on the recommended closure list of the Beeching Report, before it could even begin its second season in 1963. Already the line was running down: Washford signal box had closed in 1952; Minehead engine shed went in 1956; and the station at Norton Fitzwarren saw its last passenger on 30 October 1961. Following the announced line closure, goods traffic ceased by 6 July 1964. The last train left Minehead on Saturday 2 January 1971.

Exactly thirty-four days later, a working party led by local businessman Douglas Fear launched an investigation into the feasibility of operating this as a privately owned line. By May 1971 the new West Somerset Railway Company (WSRC) had been established with the intention of running a round-the-year commuter service, adding steam trains in the summer for the tourist trade. These were early days and while Somerset County Council helped to back the venture, the worry of failure leading to parts of the line (particularly the prime site at Minehead Station) falling into the hands of developers saw them purchase the line themselves and lease it back to the WSRC. A wise move when it soon became apparent that the commuter service was a dream too far. Yet the heritage line began to take shape and a train ran from Minehead to Blue Anchor on 28 March 1976, with Williton served from 28 August that year. Passengers could alight at Stogumber by May 1978 and Bishops Lydeard was reopened on 9 June 1979.

Organisers were quick to realise that the holiday camp at Helwell Bay, near Watchet, was a potential earner. Thus, in June 1987 a new station opened at Doniford Halt. Later, a triangle was laid out at Norton Fitzwarren, using part of the old Devon & Somerset route, and a station opened here in August 2009. With a turntable incorporated at Minehead there was now no need for locomotives to run backwards. Engines appear to drag the rolling stock when running backwards and, while there are no real problems for tank engines, it is aesthetically more pleasing to see them facing 'the right way' and pulling coaches behind them.

Great Western Railway Class 5101 2-6-2 tank engine No. 4160 is ready to pull out of Minehead. The design was unofficially known as the Large Prairie. (*Author*)

Minehead station sign with No. 4160 in the background. (*Author*)

The terminus at Minehead is in a prime location on the seafront and is the headquarters of the heritage line. When it comes to preservation the infrastructure is not quite as it was in BR days. The old station has been converted to offices and the modern ticket office blends perfectly with the original architecture. Similarly, what is now the engine shed was formerly the goods shed.

To allow traffic to use a new relief road required the construction of a new level crossing just beyond the platform, but there is a second, original crossing at Dunster West. Another entirely new construction is the carriage workshop near the far end of the platform, essential for work to be carried out in the unpredictable British climate. Minehead's signal box is an original, although it never stood here until moved by the workers from Watchet.

There was a turntable at Minehead in BR days but it was removed in 1967 as diesel electric multiple units were designed to run both ways. A replacement was acquired from Pwllheli Station: this 55ft-diameter turntable extended to 65ft (using the original GWR engineering patterns) and was installed in May 2008 as part of a £6 million redevelopment project courtesy of Somerset Council.

Just a mile and a half away is Dunster Station, itself a mile away from the village of the same name and its historic buildings; among these is Dunster Castle. Distinguished visitors arriving by railway were welcomed by a station of imposing design and not at all in keeping with its almost isolated location near the coast. It is here that the Railway Printing Company established their base in the old parcels office. From here they supply all the heritage lines in the country by printing card tickets on the old Edmondson railway ticket machine.

At Dunster goods shed a man was killed some years ago in a shunting accident and he is held to remain here, at least in spirit, as the figure whose ghostly presence has been reported on a number of occasions. One man who was particularly affected by what he saw was a former British Rail driver who, having experienced something while bringing a night train through, refused to be on the footplate of any engine coming through Dunster after dark for at least two years.

Just outside Dunster is the third level crossing in quick succession. Almost 2 miles away is Blue Anchor, with the fourth of the six level crossings on the line immediately before the platform and adjacent to the pedestrian entrance to the station itself. Originally known as Bradley Gate when it opened in 1874, it soon changed to its present name, which derives from the seventeenth-century inn which is still standing at the opposite end of the beach from the station. Here, the station buildings house a railway museum, predominantly displaying items from the GWR and its West Country lines.

Heading east for 2 miles we arrive at Washford along an incline of 1 in 65 (1.5 per cent). This may not sound particularly steep but it is approaching the limit for steam trains. Here, the Somerset & Dorset Railway Trust Museum displays an impressive collection of railwayana, including station name boards, lamps, tools, signalling equipment, tickets, photographs, and handbills, as well as the expected

At Dunster Station is the Edmondson railway ticket machine, where many of the heritage lines obtain those authentic thick card tickets. (*Courtesy of the West Somerset Railway*)

locomotives and associated rolling stock. Alongside the original stone station building is a wooden one; this houses a recreation of a signal box on the old Somerset & Dorset Joint Railway at Midford and is open to visitors.

Passing the Kenton Loop and crossing the line of the former West Somerset Mineral Railway, after another 2 miles we reach Watchet. Overlooking the small harbour, itself brimming with history and worth exploring, one can hardly fail to notice the unusual arrangement of the station. Unlike virtually every other station, this is not aligned along its length but stands at right angles to the platform and line.

It is a mere mile away to Doniford Halt which, as already noted, was an extra station opened on 27 June 1987 to serve the holiday camp which had been developed on the former Doniford army base. Although a new station, the curved platform has utilised the concrete slabs taken from Montacute on the Durston to

Yeovil branch line, while the shelter was recovered from Cove Halt on the Exe Valley Railway.

Less than three-quarters of a mile further along we arrive at Williton. Enthusiasts will instantly recognise the typical style of the Bristol & Exeter Railway station design, particularly in the Italianate chimney. The signal box dates from the same period, the only surviving example still in use. On the other side of the station building the former goods shed is used as a diesel heritage visitor centre and workshops. A recent addition, to save passengers using the level crossing, is the footbridge. Brought from Trowbridge Station, it affords good views of the line and box hedge garden beyond the platform, which is over a century old.

Stogumber, just over 3 miles from Williton, probably qualifies as the most pleasing on the eye of them all. The original stone-built buildings blend perfectly with immaculately maintained gardens. Its small size is misleading, for the nearby Railway Hotel shows this was among the busiest stops on the line during its early days.

Crowcombe Heathfield is, as evidenced below, the favoured location on the line for filmmakers over several decades. At 2½ miles from Stogumber, this station is the highest point on the line at almost 400ft above sea level. Given a Grade II listing, all that remains of the station buildings are the former living quarters: the stationmaster's house and railway workers' cottages still lived in today. The present signal box, or rather the upper half, was brought here from Ebbw Vale in 1994 and

Bishops Lydeard is the eastern end of the West Somerset Railway for passengers. (*Author*)

placed upon a newly constructed lower portion (you can clearly see the join). Reminders of the original broad gauge can be found here: the western platform has a portion of the 7ft ½in track laid out for comparison.

Bishops Lydeard was once the terminus for the heritage line, with the Quantock Belle dining car still based here. The second platform of 1906 is still used, although the facilities have extended to include a car park and shop. The original platform leads to the goods shed, itself now housing a visitor centre and museum. Highlights include the Taunton Model Railway Club layout on permanent exhibition, while the former GWR sleeping car has been beautifully restored.

Norton Fitzwarren is exactly 3 miles east of here and stands a quarter of a mile north of the original version. It does not appear on the West Somerset Railway's timetable but the single platform does serve to bring passengers further along than Bishops Lydeard to connect to specials; otherwise it serves more to assist with connections to the main line at Taunton just under a mile away. Here is a length of trackbed from the dismantled Barnstaple branch line; a ballast reclamation site was established, while sufficient room has been set aside for rolling stock and locomotive restoration depots.

Today the line has some fifty permanent staff and a volunteer workforce of around 900. In order to maintain a high degree of competence, the line asks for a minimum of fifty appearances each year from these volunteers, thus avoiding any chance of forgetfulness, complacency or ignorance of operating procedures. Obviously this is a general rule and it would be difficult to enforce as some of the volunteers come from as far away as Scotland.

A good proportion of the workforce are former British Rail staff. Whether through early retirement or as a hobby in their spare time, these individuals offer their time, skills, expertise and enthusiasm. Of course, no technical training is required; indeed, these volunteers are at least as likely to add to the collective knowledge as to learn from it. This is clearly an advantage on the engineering side, but equally valuable for less obvious areas such as signalling.

Staff are required to wear as close an approximation of the appropriate uniform as possible. In some instances this is protective and functional; in other areas it marks the office or position of the person wearing it. This applies not only to stationmaster and porter, guard and signalman, but also to refreshment room staff.

Among the visitors the staff can expect is a group of Birmingham transvestite lorry drivers, who apparently visit annually wearing their 'alternative' attire. Yet even they were not the source of two of the oddest questions asked of staff. As we have already seen, Minehead is the western terminus for trains, so east is the only possible way to go on leaving the station. Therefore, the question 'Which way does the train go when it leaves Minehead?' seems rather pointless. But it is perhaps not quite as ludicrous as the passenger who treated a member of staff to this gem, when enquiring, 'Is the line the same gauge all the way?'

As with many heritage lines, the West Somerset Railway, and particularly that around Crowcombe Heathfield, has been used by filmmakers as the backdrop to their period dramas. In 1997 the BBC filmed *The Land Girls* here and Crowcombe Heathfield appeared as Bamford Station. Rivals ITV brought David Suchet here in his role as Poirot for the episode entitled 'The Cornish Mystery'. Two years earlier, the BBC brought the production team for *The Lion, the Witch and the Wardrobe* here to film their mini-series.

A children's drama series called *The Flockton Flyer* was shot here in 1976–77. Fittingly, this told the story of a preservation railway, albeit through the actions of a group of children and not adults. *The Belstone Fox* was a 1973 film using the (then) unopened line around Crowcombe Heathfield to film a story about a fox who continually outsmarted the hounds who pursued him. But the most watched footage was also the earliest and filmed before the eventual closure. In 1964 Beatlemania came to the West Somerset Railway. The early part of the film *A Hard Day's Night* is shot on a train when the boys are introduced to Paul McCartney's troublesome grandfather ('Clean, isn't he?'), portrayed by Wilfred Bramble, as they travel to Marylebone Station in London. While their destination is certainly Marylebone, they reach it by filming scenes on this line.

Clearly such events provide a welcome and much-needed boost to the economy of the line. While few of the workers are paid, and even ignoring the

Following major restoration, No. 3850 was returned to service at the West Somerset Railway in 2011. The engine and tender are painted in the black of British Rail. (*Author*)

general maintenance costs to the infrastructure, it may come as a surprise to discover how much it costs just to run the steam engines. Every ten years the engines have to be stripped down and completely rebuilt, and the current cost for this is a little over £600,000. Even running the engine along the line is a major factor, for each engine will cover some 80 miles on a normal day and incur running expenses of £1,000 per day, and there are two engines running.

Such expenditure means the West Somerset Railway is reliant on donations for props and signs. One of the most obvious signs hangs over the doors of the sheds. This enamel sign was found in a famer's barn by his son when he inherited the property and cleaned out the shed. Local breweries have also donated advertising signs. A surprisingly significant contribution to the coffers comes from the second-hand book store on the platform. Like the refreshment room it is open all year long and, since all the books are donated, brings in excellent funding.

Among the future plans is the extension of the passing loop at Williton. The platform here is also in line for a much-needed extension because during the summer, when trains are formed of eight coaches at peak times, they are too long to fit in the station. Undoubtedly this popular line will continue to develop and, as with so many heritage lines, will evolve over time rather than through long-term plans. Ironically, this is almost how the original line developed in the mid-nineteenth century.

4   EAST SOMERSET RAILWAY

Prior to the cuts of 1963 the East Somerset ran from Witham to Wells, with connections to both the Cheddar Valley line and the Somerset & Dorset Joint Railway. Today, this 2½-mile line runs from Cranmore to Mendip Vale, visiting Merryfield Lane Halt and Cranmore West en route.

Opening on 9 November 1858 it was originally a broad gauge line carrying trains from Witham to Shepton Mallet. Four years later the line was extended to Wells and by 1874 had been acquired by the Great Western Railway and linked to its other routes, such as the Cheddar Valley line and the Bristol & Exeter Railway. This connection meant obtaining rights to run along a section of the Somerset & Dorset Joint Railway, where difficulties arose with the standard gauge. Hence, by 1892 East Somerset had been converted to 4ft 8½in. The line saw little change for the next seventy years until it was a victim of the cuts of 1963, while freight continued to bring bitumen along it until 1985.

The first indication of any preservation line was in 1972, when the famous railway and wildlife artist David Shepherd purchased Cranmore Station. Utilising a section of track between the station and his home, he ran his own locomotives: No. 92203 *Black Prince*, a 2-10-0 Class 9F; and No. 75029 *Green Knight*, a BR Standard 4 4-6-0, offering rides in a brake van the following year.

Trains terminate at Mendip Vale where a footpath is the only means of access to the station. At present this stop simply allows the passengers to watch the locomotive run round for the return journey. The next stop is at Merryfield Lane Halt, although the name should not be misunderstood: this is no request stop and almost every train stops here irrespective of whether it is heading to or from the next stop of Cranmore West.

Today, Cranmore West is only an opportunity for visitors to disembark and view the engine shed on their walk back to Cranmore Station, the hub of the railway. However, during the early days this was the terminus as British Rail's freight traffic still came through Cranmore.

The main station at Cranmore has been restored. Visitors will find a ticket office, a well-stocked museum and a period waiting room. As with Merryfield Lane Halt and Cranmore West, there is a well-designed picnic area which is particularly popular with families as it adjoins the children's play area. For those who desire a cooked meal and waitress service, a restaurant caters for most tastes, with the nearby art gallery displaying a number of works by local artists, including David Shepherd.

The line is run by a team of twenty-four volunteers who wear the uniform with pride, a uniform they will have purchased themselves. Unusually, not only the line but the vast majority of locomotives and rolling stock are owned by the heritage company. Future plans include extending the line as far as Shepton Mallet, the major stumbling block of this 2¾ miles being just one missing bridge, which should not prove much of a problem.

As with all heritage lines, one of the best sources of income is from film companies who delight in finding a ready-made period backdrop to suit whatever era they are working on at that moment. Among the scenes shot here was an advertisement for Freeserve in 2002; a documentary about the railway in 2003; an ITV drama entitled *Flash Back* in 1986; and Ian Ogilvy in the remake of *Maigret* in 1988.

Film crews are welcome but famously frustrating. With their work reliant on so many factors – weather, light, equipment, actors, writers, etc. – sticking to any sort of schedule is almost impossible. For the railway, where the timetable has to be followed rigidly, the sound of a jet aircraft overhead would not be a problem, but if filming a Victorian or Edwardian drama an instant retake would be required.

Probably the best-known film was that starring Harrison Ford and Lesley-Anne Down. A wartime story of a love triangle, *Hanover Street* featured a motorbike chase which included stunt rider Eddie Kidd leaping over a cutting at Merryfield Lane.

5   DARTMOOR RAILWAY

This is a line which parallels the Tarka Trail, a cycleway and footpath discussed in its own chapter. Another length of the line remains operational and still carries freight. Owned by Aggregate Industries Ltd, the line is maintained as part of the lease agreement with the heritage railway.

Originally, the route was part of the London & South Western Railway's West of England main line. Linking the two major cities of Exeter and Plymouth, it opened in stages between 1865 and 1879. Marked for closure, the last British Rail train ran beyond Meldon in 1968; the Exeter to Okehampton service was withdrawn four years later. For the next twenty-five years trains continued to run along this line, carrying railway ballast from Meldon Quarry, with occasional freight to the goods yard at Okehampton while it remained open.

A regular Sunday service was operated by Devon County Council from 1997 during the peak season, from the end of May to the middle of September. This service consists of five returns from Exeter's St James Park Station to Okehampton: a sensible idea for it connects with the heritage railway and the Tarka Trail. Plans to begin a regular weekday service of four trains each day were announced by Devon & Cornwall Railways Ltd in 2010. While this has yet to be approved, it remains a real possibility.

Okehampton Station. (*Author*)

A visit to the railway by a local primary school was marked by the delightful touch of a commemorative platform ticket, which the children paid for with a pre-decimal one penny piece, provided by Dartmoor Railway. (*Author*)

DARTMOOR RAILWAY

PLATFORM TICKET

PRICE Id

VALID ON
19 JUNE 2012

for access to
OKEHAMPTON STATION PLATFORMS

Date   Ticket No.

While chartered runs and specials trains were seen on rare occasions, it was not until 1997 that a regular passenger service operated once more under the banner of the Dartmoor Railway over the 15½ miles from Meldon Quarry to Coleford Junction. Operated by 2 permanent staff, 20 volunteers and another 250 members, a service is hauled by diesel engines known affectionately as Thumper for the rhythmical sound they make when idling. While the engines belong to the line, the rolling stock is on permanent loan.

Beyond Meldon Station is the viaduct of the same name, still an impressive construction. The station was never intended to be an official stop and was never shown on timetables. Very short platforms, only long enough to serve a single coach, were the only clue that Meldon Quarry Halt may also see passenger traffic. However, no passenger train ever stopped here, only a single coach at the end of the ballast train, allowing workers and their families to travel to Okehampton. At its peak some 300,000 tons of ballast were shipped from the quarry.

The original platform was replaced when Meldon became the terminus for the Dartmoor Railway in 2000. Indeed, it was constructed closer to Okehampton than the original and made to blend in with the remainder of the line. While there is no access to motor vehicles, it is well served by the so-called Granite Way, officially cycleway route number 27. A buffet car here allows views over the valley and the best opportunity to observe and photograph the viaduct.

Two miles away is Okehampton. Opened in 1871, it was an important junction for the lines to Bude, Padstow and, most importantly, Plymouth. Boat train passengers came through here from Stonehouse Pool and Plymouth, while those travelling on Atlantic Coast Express and Devon Belle prestige services also came through Okehampton.

Somewhat controversially, Okehampton was not on the list of closures in the 1963 Beeching Report. While commuters from the small town welcomed the news, those who travelled from other, busier stations cited Okehampton as an example of the many errors in the recommendations. The stay of execution

DARTMOOR RAILWAY

OKEHAMPTON STATION

COMPLIMENTARY PLATFORM TICKET

Issued 3rd June 2012

to commemorate the 40th anniversary of the last daily passenger service from Okehampton on Saturday 3rd June 1972.

Okehampton Station was opened by Devon & Cornwall Railway on 3rd October 1871. Through services to Plymouth ceased on 6th May 1968, a shuttle service to Exeter continuing until June 1972.

Similarly, the fortieth anniversary of the passenger service from Okehampton was commemorated with a ticket printed in-house by the Dartmoor Railway. (*Author*)

was short-lived, however, as British Rail closed the station in 1972. In 1997 the reopening of Okehampton Station included a model shop and cafe, and the old goods shed was refurbished as a youth hostel and activity centre.

The future of Okehampton seems assured for several reasons: first, First Great Western continue to run those Sunday trains from Exeter; second, as detailed below, the heritage railway seems destined to expand its service; third, a purpose-built railhead at Okehampton is planned to serve the timber industry, replacing a thousand lorry journeys every week of the year; and fourth, reopening the route through Bere Alston would provide an alternative route through to Plymouth and Cornwall should engineering work or storms make the sea wall around Dawlish impassable. Furthermore, should the Dawlish line be abandoned as being too expensive to maintain, a ready-made viable alternative would prove an invaluable money-spinner.

Just under 4 miles further on is Sampford Courtenay. Originally known as Okehampton Road, until the line was extended as far as Okehampton and it became Belstone Corner, some records suggest the present station name is not exactly how it first appeared. Doubtless the village is Sampford Courtenay, yet early records of the station seem to suggest this was Sampford Courtney. This may be a recording error; surviving images of the station neither confirm nor disprove this alternative spelling, although there is evidence of the railway's incorrect spelling becoming the norm. Not far away at Paignton is the perfect example for, until the coming of the railway, the spelling was Paington.

Plans are at an advanced stage to reopen the line as far as Yeoford. Presumably this will involve reopening stations at North Tawton, 3 miles from Sampford Courtenay, and at Bow, another 3 miles along. Both were closed in 1972 by British Rail. Yeoford and Coleford Junction are where the Dartmoor Railway connects with the Tarka line. Described as a 'community railway', the service continues to grow. In the last ten years annual passenger numbers have more than doubled to reach 13,000 in 2011.

To provide a connection with the Dartmoor Railway requires the reopening of the disused platform at Yeoford. At the time of writing, delays were continuing

Sampford Courtenay Station sign.
(*Author*)

over the transfer of the line and buildings between the old and new owners. It seems inevitable that passenger numbers on both lines will increase when they complement one other with synchronised timetables and services.

While the heritage factor will always be uppermost in their thoughts, the Dartmoor Railway aims to provide a regular service all year round. Opening up Okehampton East is next on the agenda. While this station is on the outskirts and removed from all but the edge of the developed area, its intention is to act more as a park and ride, keeping the traffic out of Okehampton and taking people on to Exeter.

For those travelling the Dartmoor Railway today the views are quite superb. Delights await the family and the most ardent railway buff, the latter doubtless already aware that Meldon Station is the highest in southern England. From here walkers can reach the Dartmoor National Park to take in views of Yes Tor and High Willhays. One of the most popular journeys is the dinner train, an evening special run between Okehampton and Coleford. Normally everything runs like clockwork: staff serve the main course on the outward journey, with dessert and coffee on the return. However, one evening the catering staff suddenly realised there was no milk for the coffee.

Unbeknown to the passengers, who were still savouring the taste of their dessert, their stop at the bridge in North Tawton was in no way routine. A volunteer, who was expected to do nothing but offer a hand to serving, found himself feeling his way in the dark along the track to seek out the edge of the bridge. From here it was a hazardous descent down a steep bank lined with brambles to reach the road and the Station Hotel public house. Having procured two or three cartons of milk for the coffee, he made the even more difficult journey back up the bank and along the line to the train. If passengers noticed his somewhat dishevelled appearance on his return, none commented; nor were they ever made aware of his heroic journey in the blackness to ensure the paying customer had a choice of black or white coffee.

6   AVON VALLEY RAILWAY

This story goes back to 1869 and the opening of the Mangotsfield and Bath branch line, enabling Bath to be connected to the Midland Railway Network. Essentially a local service, it also connected with trains from the Midlands, Bristol and the increasingly popular holiday destinations on the Somerset & Dorset Joint Railway.

Almost a century later we come to 6 March 1966, when the final passenger train ran along this line, a victim of the Beeching cuts. As with many other heritage lines, the tracks were ripped up and the buildings boarded up; but in 1972 the first steps were taken to reopen this former branch line. It eventually became known as the Avon Valley Railway: 3 miles of line which is now a popular tourist attraction, for it also links to leisure boats on the Avon, and a network of cycleways and footpaths.

When the first engines ran along the reopened track it was just 100yd long. Over the years the line grew to become what it is today. One major landmark was the extension which opened in 1991, when the part of the line between Bitton Station and Oldland Common was completed. At the opening ceremony were three special guests of honour: driver Archie Gunning, fireman Albert Parsons and guard Bernard Ware, who formed the crew on the last scheduled British Rail service twenty-five years ago to the very day.

The line ran into difficulties in 1988 when the extension was challenged by a few local residents who objected to engines running past their homes. An expensive court case followed, which saw £30,000 in funding disappear in legal fees when it should have been used for the benefit of the railway. Victorious in the court case, the line has enjoyed great success ever since.

Assisted by a veritable army of volunteers is a nucleus of fifteen or so permanent full-time employees. These people take great pride in wearing the uniforms required by the strict dress code in operation. Together they are justifiably proud of being awarded the Queen's Award for Volunteers, the group volunteer equivalent of the MBE.

At the beginning of the twenty-first century a most ambitious project was undertaken with the full support of the South Gloucestershire Council. The building of another quarter of a mile of track meant crossing the Avon and bringing the railway to the river, where the timing of the trains would coincide with a completely new venture offering river trips along the Avon aboard the *River Princess*. This also meant building a brand-new station named Avon Riverside, which included a 50ft-long landing stage where boats could tie up.

It could be considered a unique event to see a new station being built on a heritage line; most are refurbished or copies of earlier buildings, as authenticity is of vital importance. However, here the architecture had to fit in with the rest of the line, while also being functional. On the opposite end of the line is Oldland Common Station, which was built in 1935 to serve the growing population. The platforms were constructed from railway sleepers and, while it did once have a small ticket office, it became first an unstaffed halt in 1964 and eventually closed in 1966, reopening in 1991.

It is Bitton, however, which is the focal point of the line. There is another new building here – the buffet – which also fits in with the restored buildings. The yard houses rolling stock and covered workshops where repairs and restoration is carried out by an army of volunteers.

It is here that the line connects to the Bristol and Bath Railway Path. As the name suggests, this is the former line which connected the cities of Bristol and Bath. With the track lifted and the bed surfaced, this route covers 13 miles with hardly an incline. This was the brainchild of Sustrans, a charity dedicated to providing a network of sustainable transport, and this was their first venture. Again, this was a route created by the Beeching closures and, as Bitton lies midway along the path, we shall pick up the route at Bristol.

Bitton Station sign.
(*Author*)

K186 industrial shunter at Bitton. (*Courtesy of the Avon Valley Railway*)

Work started on this path in 1979 and was completed seven years later. It connects to other paths and detours to points of interest which, together with the Avon Valley Railway, Avon boat trips and the Kennet & Avon Canal, makes for a variety of interests to suit many tastes. Picking up the route at its starting point at St Philips Road, off Midland Road which was named after the Midland Railway, we head north-east and soon come to Lawrence Hill Station, where trains still run.

Passing through Easton and Fishponds we reach Staple Hill; here the former station area provides a picnic site before the track heads under the hill itself through the tunnel. Approximately 500yd long, it is illuminated and the refuges have been filled in so no unwanted surprises lie in wait. One former resident of Staple Hill was Bob Bateman, an evangelist preacher who died on 14 April 1912. If this date sounds familiar, it is because it was the day that RMS *Titanic* sank on its maiden voyage. One of the most poignant stories of the sinking is about how the ship's orchestra played *Abide with Me* as the waters closed around them. The conductor for that special service on that evening was none other than Bob Bateman.

Shortly afterwards we arrive at the old Mangotsfield Station. It was this station which proved the inspiration for Arnold Ridley's *Ghost Train*. As many will be aware, Arnold Ridley, who played Private Godfrey, the oldest member of the platoon in *Dad's Army*, also wrote this play, later adapted for the big screen and starring Arthur Askey, Richard Murdoch and Kathleen Harrison. Ridley's early ambition to be an actor foundered as a result of injuries received on active duty during the First World War. Having missed his connection, Ridley was delayed at Mangotsfield when he heard a train approaching. Despite the sound of the train telling him it was passing through the station, there was no sight of it. There is an explanation, however: the acoustics were deceptive and he was hearing a train passing behind the chocolate factory on another line.

Here the cycle path splits: the Avon Cycleway heads north to the left, while we turn right and to the south. The traffic signals on London Road mark the point where, for those interested, there is a short detour to see Kingswood Museum, which tells the story of coal mining in the area, features the building which housed the old pin factory, and contains the Warmley Giant (a huge representation of Neptune), gardens and grottoes, all of which are associated with the entrepreneur William Champion. Warmley Station still provides refreshments for those who require them, every day in the summer and at most weekends in the winter months. The next stop on the old line also provides food and drink almost every day of the year.

That next station is Bitton which connects to the Avon Valley Railway and Avon Valley Country Park. Thus we continue to Saltford, with its brass mills, and on to Kelston. Here the station, servicing both Kelston and Saltford, has been demolished. The land around was owned by Inigo Jones, who only gave

A diesel-hauled service waiting to pull out of Bitton Station. (*Author*)

permission for the station to be built on condition it served Kelston village. However, there is no road access and passengers were obliged to walk. Jones did not stop there; he insisted he should be allowed to stop any Midland train to either board or leave the carriage himself, providing he gave a full day's notice. Furthermore, it is said he also insisted the station should never close.

From here the route takes us to Bath, running parallel to the present railway, a remnant of the GWR line, itself the foremost reason the route between the two cities was closed. Arriving at Pulteney Bridge, there are links north to the Cotswold Way and south along the Kennet & Avon Canal.

The day this author visited was, quite coincidentally, the same time the Take 2 Film Company was shooting a children's drama for the BBC. At the time the series was still untitled, although a steam train was clearly part of the plot and one of the vans had been transformed into (of all things) a futuristic disco!

Those who work this line see themselves as a family unit. Those who come in at the bottom will put in many years of service and they are proud of their successes in nurturing apprentices. One new appointment was a buffet manager who had been a prize winner in her earlier catering career. This high standard has resulted in many bookings for children's birthday parties, and the Fish and Chip Evenings are among the most popular events. Another 'special' is the Murder Mysteries put on by Murder in Mind of Berkshire. Perhaps the greatest compliment that can be paid to the enthusiasts, who take great care with their attire, is that it is often impossible for staff to distinguish between the actors and the paying customers.

The enthusiasm of the staff is epitomised by the story of one young man who, contrary to his parents' aspirations, approached the Avon Valley Railway with a view to receiving an apprenticeship and eventual employment in the engineering sheds. They agreed to his request on the proviso that he arranged his own sponsorship. Perhaps they never thought they would hear from him again, but within a week he was back and armed with a letter which put him as an apprentice toolmaker first at Rolls-Royce and then at Dorothea Restorations. Having been through the apprenticeship he achieved his goal of a full-time position, yet perhaps even the young Marcus Cowley could not have foreseen his current position of yard manager.

Plans to extend the line as far as Saltford have been a real target ever since the bridge was constructed at Avon Riverside. Indeed, the rails have already been acquired and await installation as soon as permission is obtained. Not that this will be done overnight; a lead time of some three to four years is realistic. These rails cost the Avon Valley Railway £5,000, a sizable sum of money which only covered the cost of delivering this huge amount of metal. The rails themselves were donated to the line.

There may be only one heritage line but it is operated by two bodies. The infrastructure comes under one body, while the rolling stock is mainly owned by the Avon Heritage Railway Trust, a registered charity. Some coaching is also privately owned and part of members' collections.

Visitors come on foot, on public transport, in their cars and in organised coach parties. When they arrive they are greeted on the coach before disembarking. The guide gives a brief history of the heritage line and this, of course, includes news of its closure in the 1960s. At the mention of the name Richard Beeching, the coach parties always respond with a chorus of 'Boo!'

7 MID-NORFOLK RAILWAY

Mention Beeching and thoughts turn to steam. However, we should remember that the rationalisation of Britain's railways had nothing to do with the mode of power or indeed the design and splendour of the engine. To turn the nationalised industry into a profitable organisation was not related to the abolition of steam; that decision had been made by British Rail years before. The move was from steam to the more efficient diesel and electricity, and, while there is no nostalgic link between Beeching and the pantograph, diesel heritage railways are more popular than the layman would think.

This line is an interesting Beeching casualty, for it is one of those now often described as a 'new generation' heritage railway and not only does it provide a leisure service, but also gives something back to the modern railway system. Over 11 miles in length, it is predominantly used for tourism and runs diesel services, although the occasional steam locomotive is run. From time to time commercial freight services also operate, while the main-line companies utilise this stretch for training their employees.

Preservation started in 1974, although the first passenger service did not operate until 1995. It utilises the southern section of the line serving Wymondham, Dereham, Fakenham and Wells-next-the-Sea opened by the Norfolk Railway in 1847. The old station sign can be seen in the line's museum at Dereham. Note how, yet again, the railway's attention to detail was not what it should have been as Wells station was named Wells-on-Sea. The Beeching cuts closed the line to passengers over a five-year period beginning in 1964, although a freight service was to continue until 1989.

Much as the line was closed in stages, its beginnings saw a similar pattern between 1847 and 1857, eventually becoming part of the Great Eastern Railway in 1862 with the company paying for the double track from Wymondham to Dereham. With the railways eventually becoming the 'Big Four', this branch line came under the control of the London & North Eastern Railway in 1923.

During both world wars the military presence in the east of England, in particular the RAF, saw new sidings at Dereham as the Air Ministry built more airfields. The nationalisation of the railways following the end of the Second World War brought a quick closure to the small branch between County School and Wroxham, albeit only to passengers, with that between Dereham and Wells the first to suffer in October 1964.

As heritage railways go, the Mid-Norfolk Railway had rather strange beginnings. In 1973 the country was facing an oil crisis and a meeting was called at Dereham the following year. The Railway Development Society petitioned to restore the passenger service from Dereham to Wymondham – remember the track was still *in situ* – to alleviate commuter problems caused by the shortage of petrol. British Rail would have done so on payment of £247,000, but this was rejected by Norfolk County Council.

The petitioners were not to be deterred, however, and continued under their new name of the Wymondham, Dereham & Fakenham Railway Action Committee. Four years later another meeting with Norfolk County Council representatives marked the real beginning of this heritage railway.

While the stations closed and train services ceased to operate, neither track nor the few buildings at Dereham were cleared. This provided ample parking space and today the yard contains locomotives and rolling stock located at Dereham by

Dereham Station. (*Author*)

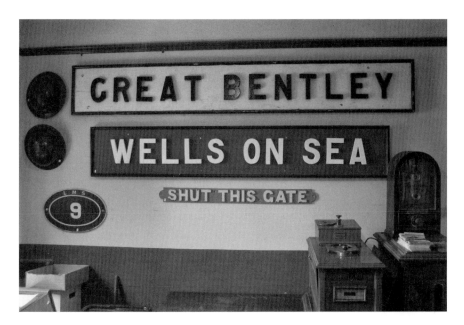

Old railway signs are on display in the museum at Dereham. Note the sign that says Wells-on-Sea, when the station's place name was actually Wells-next-the-Sea. (*Author*)

the societies and enthusiasts who own them. The Mid-Norfolk Railway owns none of these; their owners clearly prefer to see them working on the line.

Today's success must have been a distant dream in the early days. In 1980 the team failed to preserve the Ryburgh to Fakenham section of the line and, three years later, had leased Hadingham Station to open up the goods yard. A Ruston 0-4-0 diesel locomotive was the beginning of a small heritage centre, but it soon became clear income was falling well short of basics, such as rent and rates. Thus, after three years they moved to Yaxham, a move forced by the auctioning off of Hadingham.

The following year fortunes seemed to be taking an upturn. Breckland District Council purchased County School and granted the society a 999-year lease on the site where they were invited to lay track. It was seen as an opportunity to connect to the British Rail line at North Elmham and to the charter trains which ran here. Nevertheless, this was abandoned two years later when this line was closed. This was not as disastrous as it would appear for it effectively isolated the heritage line, making development easier with a clean slate, and resulted in the Mid-Norfolk Railway Society's creation in 1990, a year after the Great Eastern Railway.

With the addition of half a mile of track towards North Elmham, the County School site run by the Great Eastern Railway ran its first passenger train on 2 November 1991. This train consisted of an old converted brake coach and an industrial diesel locomotive. By 1993 it was hoped to run a regular passenger service used by some 400 commuters every weekday, with weekend excursions including shopping trips to London and trips to the seaside in summer. Furthermore, the planned hotel and shopping centre would produce much-needed revenue.

For a while the two bodies worked well together. However, the Great Eastern Railway's plans were overly optimistic (to say the least!) and when plans were announced to lift the line from Dereham to Wymondham, the two bodies effectively became competitors. Hence the Mid-Norfolk took steps to announce their own plans for the line, which were approved by British Rail in 1994, albeit on a temporary basis and likely encouraged by the increasing problem of vandalism. After a series of legal and financial hiccoughs, the Mid-Norfolk Railway Preservation Trust was entrusted with restoring the line, equipment and rolling stock, operating a regular passenger service, and replacing or renovating associated architecture and landscaping. By August 1995 two diesel locomotives and five coaches were stationed at the temporary base at Yaxham and, with the construction of a temporary halt at Dereham on the Rash's Green Industrial Estate, trains began to operate along this stretch from 23 December 1995.

On 11 April 1998 the sale of the route from Wymondham to Dereham was completed. A price of £100,000 included the buildings and goods area at Dereham, with a further £25,000 securing the 4½ miles of line from Dereham to North Elmham. Having also secured an agreement with Breckland District Council to take over the station and trackbed at County School, after a long and hard struggle, the Mid-Norfolk Railway Preservation Trust was in business.

A passenger service between Dereham and Wymondham began on 2 May 1999 with the opening of Wymondham Abbey Station. This remains the southern terminus of the passenger line, although the track continues to join the Breckland line. Passengers wishing to change between the two need to make their own way between the lines, a distance of about a mile.

Kimberley Park began as a single platform, but a second was constructed when the line was doubled up in the 1880s. With glass-fronted buildings and canopies this must have been an attractive example of a Victorian village railway station. The buildings and goods yard are still here, but both are privately owned while the platform has been retained for local use. Still clearly visible is the original Great Eastern Railway signal box, although there are plans to replace this with a cabin from Soham in order to make it operational once more.

Thuxton was originally a request stop but given full status from 16 June 2002. The waiting rooms no longer serve their original purpose but, now privately owned, have been restored as holiday accommodation. It has two platforms, the second retained to serve the passing loop, and a single siding for goods. The modern signal box, south of the level crossing, is modelled on the design at Shippea Hill in Cambridgeshire. The original, located north of the station, was downgraded to a ground frame in 1933 and the box itself was demolished in 1955.

A train shortly before departure from Dereham heading for Wymondham Abbey. (*Author*)

A temporary sign at Wymondham Abbey Station. (*Author*)

Yaxham is the only station on the line which has remained largely unchanged. The original signal box, although not owned by the Mid-Norfolk Railway, still stands on the platform, although its lever frame has long been removed. The stationmaster's house and station hotel, too, are today privately owned. Shelters on the up platform have been refurbished.

That many of these buildings have been saved is largely down to one man: Mr D.C. Potter. He opened a narrow gauge railway in the former goods yard in 1967. The Hunslet 0-4-0ST *Cackler* which ran here is now working the nearby Yaxham Light Railway, while the disused lines can still be seen.

Dereham Station once served as a car showroom; the ample car parking area today used by visitors once had lines of cars for sale. The owners kept the building in excellent condition, even repainting the interior in its original green and cream. They should be further complimented on keeping the wooden canopy over the platform. Dereham suffers from a lack of buildings, particularly maintenance sheds for cover.

Dereham is the present terminus, although work progresses in opening the line towards County School and Fakenham. When this opens it will give a line of 17 miles, the third-longest heritage line in Britain. There is also the new halt at Wymondham and the erection of a maintenance shed in the yard at Dereham

Former railway buildings on the line now serve as private residences. (*Author*)

for much-needed cover. Furthermore, it seems inevitable that National Rail will eventually link to the heritage line as part of the Norfolk Orbital Railway scheme, although nothing official exists at the time of writing.

The goods shed stores and restores both locomotives and rolling stock. The installation of a footbridge brought here from Whittlesford is in the planning stage, although just when it will be in service is not yet clear. Of the four original signal boxes, two have been rebuilt and the others brought here from as far afield as Lowestoft.

The line is currently operated by a regular team of 150 or so volunteers and supported by a growing membership currently standing at around 1,000. None of the locomotives and rolling stock is owned by the line but is on permanent loan from societies who, quite rightly, desire to see their prized possessions in operation rather than standing in a museum or shed.

Thankfully, the Mid-Norfolk Railway is one of those heritage lines which continue to use the old card tickets that were once used everywhere. These are not obtained from the usual source at Dunster on the West Somerset Railway, but from a gentleman who just happened to purchase both the printing machine and the plates some years ago for what he thought might be a good investment. Hence the tickets travel all the way from the Isle of Mull!

As with many heritage lines, the Mid-Norfolk Railway offers producers and directors an excellent backdrop for period dramas. Programmes filmed here include *Weavers Green*, a soap opera made by Anglia Television, and the classic BBC comedy *'Allo 'Allo*, in which County School Station doubled as the Gare de Nouvion in the penultimate episode.

In 2004 County School Station posed as Thetford Station in a documentary about American troops of the Second World War. The film *Peter Warlock: Some Little Joy*, based on the life of composer Philip Heseltine, was also shot here. The surprisingly popular series *Great British Railway Journeys* saw former Cabinet minister Michael Portillo filming on the line in 2010. While in 2012, Dereham was used for a musical production of *The Railway Children*.

8 NENE VALLEY RAILWAY

In 1845 the London & Birmingham Railway was given the opportunity to provide a line from Blisworth through to Peterborough. Completed two years later, this was of little national significance until the late nineteenth century, when it was absorbed by the London & North Western Railway (LNWR), with later influences from the Great Northern Railway and the Midland Railway making Wansford an important junction.

From then until closure in the 1960s this was an important link between the northern parts of East Anglia and the Midlands. Closure as a passenger line was relatively late, services to Northampton ending in 1964 and to Rugby in 1966, although freight continued to use this stretch until 1972. Two years later the line was purchased by the Peterborough Development Corporation and reopened as the Nene Valley Railway (NVR) in 1977, with further extensions in 1986 and 2007 increasing the size of the heritage line to 7½ miles.

The late closure of the line created problems for the preservation railway which followed. By the time the idea of the Nene Valley Railway was becoming a reality, most of British Rail's old stocks had been appropriated by other lines and only rusting hulks remained. Hence it was not until three locomotives were acquired from the Continent – one from France and two from Sweden – that the project finally got off the ground. This led to the demolition of a bridge and alterations to a platform in order to accommodate the bigger dimensions of these engines.

Any working railway needs rolling stock and this could not be brought in until a quarter of a mile of missing track was relaid on the Fletton Loop. This was completed in March 1974, allowing the public to watch the first train run at Easter that year from Wansford to Orton Mere.

At Wansford is the Barnwell Building, moved from Barnwell Station in 1977 and originally built in 1884 to allow royal visitors to alight when visiting Barnwell Manor, home of the Duke of Gloucester. The major station building here is not the original; indeed, it was only completed in 1995 but blends perfectly as it is of

Nene Valley Railway has a good selection of Continental locomotives …

typical LNWR design. The original building is on a different platform, built in 1844 in the Jacobean style, and currently does not belong to the heritage railway, but plans are in place to bring this into their ownership.

The signal box is of a similar design. It dates from 1907 and, with over sixty levers, is one of the largest preserved boxes in the country. We also find the turntable, brought here from Bourne in Lincolnshire, not as a result of the Beeching closures but for use on the railway at Peterborough where it turned the Travelling Post Office. It was just 60ft in diameter when brought to Wansford and had to be extended by another 7ft to cope with the traffic. There is also a model railway in a former coach: three layouts have been assembled by enthusiasts, including a small layout cleverly named Iron Sidings which is displayed on top of an old ironing board!

From Wansford the line passes the Old Great North Road via a level crossing. The old connection to the Great Northern Railway to Stamford heads off shortly afterwards, and then we arrive at the former station of Castor. Little of Castor Station remains, for it closed well before the rest of the line. The next stop on the line was Orton Waterville, but today the stop is nearby at what is now known as Ferry Meadows. The new station building was brought here brick by brick from Fletton Junction. There are further plans to develop this part of the line, with a museum of Travelling Post Offices and memorabilia, including the only surviving part of the mail train made famous by the Great Train Robbery of 8 August 1963.

... and rolling stock at Wansford. (*Author*)

Today, Orton Mere provides access to Nene Park, a country park with three lakes, three children's play areas and a miniature railway. This was the original terminus for the line and was extended in the early 1980s to Peterborough Nene Valley, opening for the Spring Bank Holiday of May 1986. In the last ten years there has been speculation about the line being linked through Nene Park, across the river which gave the line its name and joining up with the present main-line station in Peterborough.

There has been another extension at the opposite end of the line from Wansford to Yarwell Junction, which was opened in 2007. This is not a refurbished station; there had never been a stop here previously. Indeed, the track had to be realigned in order to make room for the new platform, which is reached as the line emerges from the 616yd-long Wansford Tunnel which passes beneath the hamlet of Sibson. There are footpaths to this new station but no vehicular access.

Over the route between Wansford and Yarwell only is run a Hudswell Clarke 0-6-0T No. 1800. This otherwise unremarkable locomotive has achieved

The signal box at Orton Mere. (*Author*)

Orton Mere Station. (*Author*)

immortality, for in 1971 it was officially named Thomas by the Rev. W. Awdry, creator of the *Railway Series* of books – today better known as *Thomas the Tank Engine and Friends*. The line also boasts an excellent collection of Continental vehicles: a German tank engine; a similar Danish locomotive; and surplus rolling stock from Sweden.

The line is also responsible for overhauling and restoring locomotives: not just steam but diesel, too. Many more locomotives than are currently either working or on show at the NVR have been released to other lines and museums. Such work brings in much-needed revenue, especially at times when visitor numbers would not make the line a financially viable proposition.

Money is also raised by allowing filming to take place here: two James Bond films include scenes shot on these tracks – *Octopussy* and *GoldenEye*; the BBC brought their cameras to film a scene from the long-running series *Casualty*; episodes of *Secret Army* were filmed here; Hollywood producers arrived in 2008 to film *Nine* with Penelope Cruz and Daniel Day-Lewis; ITV came in 2009 to remake *Murder on the Orient Express*; a level crossing cliffhanger was shot for *EastEnders* in 2010; and a series on modes of transport for the Discovery Channel fronted by Chris Barrie was based around the Wansford site and was recently aired on Channel 5.

Locomotives in the yard at Wansford. (*Author*)

The music business has also taken advantage of what the railway has to offer. In September 1989 rock legends Queen made a video to accompany the track 'Breakthru' from their album *The Miracle*, which used an engine from Didcot, since renamed Miracle Express.

There are not only commercial ventures for the trains but private hire, too. A social group known as the Purple Ladies – so called for the predominant colour of their attire – once had afternoon tea on a trip, while a party from Tesco dressed up as characters from the *Harry Potter* books and films and turned a carriage into the Hogwarts Express for their staff Christmas party.

Other visitors were uninvited. The last stationmaster at Wansford had a cat, apparently known as Snowy. When out looking for his missing moggy one night, he ventured into Yarwell Tunnel where he was sadly struck and killed by a train. The cat is said to still wander the station looking for its master. Other ghostly sightings have included workers walking through the tunnel, a passenger on the platform, doors opening of their own volition, and what was described as 'a certain something' around the yard.

Today, a permanent staff of around twenty are supplemented by ten times that number of regular volunteers. Another 150 or so, whose talents and skills are very specific, appear at specialist events, such as the Santa Specials in the Yuletide period. Together, these see over 60,000 visitors a year on operating days alone;

there are also untold numbers who visit outside these times to view the yards, locomotives, rolling stock, buildings, and enjoy the hospitality of the station buffet, which offers catering services most days.

As with most heritage lines, card tickets are printed to fit with the period. However, these are expensive to produce, coming from the only known alternative to the Edmondson railway ticket machine at Dunster Station on the Isle of Mull; hence the normal services use a computerised printed ticket system.

With a reasonable length of line, a good selection of locomotives and rolling stock, and the line running through excellent scenery, the imagination and aspirations of the staff are clearly taking this line forward. The future certainly seems rosy indeed.

9   NORTH YORKSHIRE MOORS RAILWAY

Begun in 1836 as the Whitby & Pickering Railway, this line had been planned by the legendary George Stephenson. Originally meant to bring the produce from the important port of Whitby inland, it features the 120yd Grosmont Horse Tunnel, believed to be the oldest railway tunnel in the world.

The line carried 10,000 tons of stone to Whitby in its first year, together with 6,000 paying passengers. This route would have brought panic to the health and safety officers of today, for although the two-and-a-half-hour journey cost one shilling and threepence for a seat inside the coach, passengers paying the reduced rate of one shilling were allowed to find a seat on the roof of the carriage!

By 1845 the York & North Midland Railway had acquired the line; this was when the stations and other buildings were constructed which can still be seen today. As the numerous private railway companies began to combine, this line became part of the North Eastern Railway in 1854. In 1923 it became the London & North Eastern Railway and in 1948 it was the domain of British Rail until closure by the Beeching Report in 1965. Note that the Beck Hole Incline, a part of the original route, was not served by a steam locomotive: carriages had to be hauled up on a rope. In the early 1860s this was bypassed along the modern line but the original route is now a popular walk known as the Historic Rail Trail.

The main revenue of the railway in the early days came from transporting mineral ore, but by the 1930s that had gone. It was gradually replaced by the transportation of animal feeds. At one time there was at least one train every day carrying such cargo for distribution from these stations.

While the stations were well located to serve farms, they were not well positioned for passengers from the villages themselves. For example, at Levisham the station stands in an idyllic location in the valley bottom, while the village lies way above on a slope negotiated via a gradient in parts of 1 in 3 (33 per cent displayed in the modern usage). The thought of walking up this long incline after a hard day's work in the summer months would be bad enough, but in the depths of winter with no illumination to guide the way it would be enough to make anyone think twice.

Still, many did travel this line. In conversation with John Hardy – a man who knows this line as well as anyone having worked it for many years – he revealed the line reached its peak on a day in 1938. On that single day an amazing ninety-one trains travelled between Whitby and West Cliff – and this meant trains travelling in opposite directions negotiating a single track, an impressive piece of planning and signalling.

Two years after closure one man, Tom Salmon, led a campaign to bring about the revival of this historic railway. Together with a small band who longed to see the Grosmont to Pickering stretch of the line brought back to life, he took the first of many small steps. Great dedication and a considerable amount of hard work saw volunteers produce the occasional Steam Gala which ran steam trains for members only (insurance issues meant it could not be opened to the public at this stage).

Few heritage railway ventures avoid opposition from builders and local councils. The lines, stations and goods yards often occupied prime sites which readily lent themselves to development. In this regard North Riding County Council was most helpful, putting no barriers in the way. To balance this Pickering was already

Levisham Station. (*Author*)

planning to develop the land. Indeed, any thought of an extension to Malton evaporated when houses quickly grew across the remains of the line.

As the band grew they became a charity, thus preventing anyone from taking over the line purely for profit, and a few individuals became full time paid employees. From humble beginnings in 1972, the North Yorkshire Moors Railway (NYMR) has grown to employ eighty-five full-time and another fifty or so part-time staff during the busy summer months, with a small army of 525 registered volunteers ever ready to lend a willing hand. Uniforms for full-time staff are provided out of a uniform allowance paid by the railway. Volunteers provide their own uniforms. A broad guide to uniform requirements is well documented, but there is some latitude allowed. The company has now issued a recommended uniform catalogue for volunteers and staff.

As with all heritage lines, the need for manpower is greater than it ever was for the national railway: spares are no longer waiting on a storeman's shelf; maintenance sheds are not available at the engineering works in York or Doncaster; there are no ranks of secretaries and clerks to back local administrators who can be reached by a simple telephone call; neither is there a railway printers, or tailors and haberdashers to provide the uniforms and outfits, paperwork and paraphernalia. Since 1967 everything has had to be sourced in-house, often made by hand, with no support infrastructure.

One story emerged from a time when the *Green Arrow* required a replacement connecting rod. This Sir Nigel Gresley-designed LNER Class V2 2-6-2 locomotive No. 4771 was built in June 1936, the first of its class and the only surviving example of its kind. Although no longer in use, currently standing as a static exhibit at the National Railway Museum at York, its final runs were as part of the LNER gala on the NYMR.

When the *Green Arrow* arrived it was discovered a new connecting rod was required for the middle cylinder. Enquiries were initially made by word of mouth as it is surprising how often someone has seen or heard of something ideally suited to the task. As it happened, a shop foreman had just such a part at home – being employed as a foot rest under a desk!

While the line originally linked up to the Malton to Scarborough line at Rillington Junction, this track was lifted years ago and the current terminus is the recently restored Pickering Station. However, do not expect a modern railway station; it has been faithfully reproduced as it appeared in 1937. This period style will be seen again and again, for each station represents a different era in the history of the line. The fixtures and fittings in the offices and tea room are original, while the turntable feeds the workshops for the railways carriages. Each and every station has a different theme, and the colours, decor and design are faithfully reproduced and maintained. The period for each station was established early on in the heritage line's history, and great pride and attention to detail is taken by staff and volunteers in preserving the authenticity in each example.

During the preparation for this book, a visit to Pickering was made in the week leading up to Queen Elizabeth II's Diamond Jubilee. The flags and bunting were not out of place at Pickering Station for its 1937 theme fits another royal celebration – the Silver Jubilee of King George V, which fell in that very year.

On what was once platform two is a new exhibition venue called Train of Thought, a learning centre with a delightful interpretation of the railways of yesteryear. However, it is the attention to detail in the restored station buildings that is most impressive; that they blend in so well is a true testimony to the staff.

There was an earlier station at Pickering in use for ten years from 1836 and was found just north of the current station. Virtually all traces of this vanished when the York & North Midland Railway built the current station from 1846. Between 1973 and 1975 the NYMR used a temporary station situated just north of the current Pickering Station at High Mill while a dispute over planning consents for the current station were resolved. The train shed roof of Pickering Station, removed in 1952, was reinstated in 2011.

Within three-quarters of a mile we come to two level crossings in quick succession: High Mill followed by New Bridge. The line then swings east for 2 miles before looping north once more, through Farwarth and the delights of the North Yorkshire Moors to Levisham just over 4 miles from Pickering. Levisham

Pickering Station, ready for the Diamond Jubilee celebrations of Queen Elizabeth II. (*Author*)

is one of the stations which has a camping coach – an old carriage refurbished to provide self-catering accommodation for holidaymakers and particularly suitable for those intent on enjoying the delights of the countryside on foot.

The station itself is styled for the year 1912 and includes a carriage showing its history. It is not easy to reach because there is only a single hill road for vehicles, although there are a number of tracks and trails accessible by bike and on foot. There is also a resident artist here, Christopher Ware, whose studio is open during the busiest periods.

By the time the preservation group saw Levisham, there was little left that could be utilised. Signals had been removed or scrapped, the signal box gutted, point rodding cut up and left where it fell, buildings let out temporarily, and the lamp house burned down. A small band of hardy souls broke away from the main group and set about resurrecting the station. Due to its relative inaccessibility they opted to sleep here overnight, but the accommodation hardly justified the word. With sleeping bags on the floor of the signal box and polythene covering the broken windows, camping would have been positively palatial in comparison. Evicting rats, repairing fences and clearing ditches at least protected the station from further damage, but even by the time the first train came through in 1973, the place was unrecognisable from what we see today.

The shorter platform was the only one in use, signals had yet not been replaced, there was only a loop to allow the engine to join the front end of the train on the single track, and the level crossing was neither level nor a true crossing but a rapidly deteriorating assemblage of old railway sleepers. Many of the buildings were still being leased for alternative purposes or completely unfit for use. Although there are numerous projects still to be undertaken, the change over the intervening thirty-seven years since the first train is simply stunning.

A distance of just over 3 miles north and, having negotiated another level crossing, we come to the newly built Newton Dale Halt. This request stop, where passengers wishing to alight have to give instructions to the guard when boarding the train and passengers wishing to board must give a clear signal to the driver, has no access by road. The station was never a casualty of the Beeching cuts for it was never a station on the original railway; it has been created for walkers to access four clearly marked routes set out across the National Park aided by the Forestry Commission. Other public footpaths leading from here are not marked, but for experienced walkers with a good map there are a number to choose from. Some of the routes are suitable for cyclists and are clearly marked as such.

Materials to construct the Newton Dale Halt were brought here from Warrenby Halt, a small wooden-built station near Redcar. Only one of the platforms was used and the tiny shelter was not part of it. This was an entirely new NYMR construction in 2005 and based on the design at the Sledmere & Fimber Station on the Malton & Driffield Railway, albeit smaller and without vulnerable windows.

Another 5 miles and, shortly before Goathland, the line shows evidence of a branch. In fact, this was the original trackbed of the Whitby & Pickering Railway and lasted for some thirty years until the North Eastern Railway built the present line, a flatter route which follows the valley of the Eller Beck more closely and avoided the Beck Hole Incline. This original station was known as Goathland Station, while the new station became Goathland Mill to avoid confusion. Little

The view from the footbridge at Levisham Station, looking along the cutting to the north of Goathland. (*Author*)

remains of the buildings on the original line, although Ash Tree Cottage at the top of the incline is thought to be the overseer's cottage. Those who take the rail trail along the 3½ miles of the original line to Grosmont will be able to see this private dwelling.

The present station is today known as simply Goathland and has been recreated by the NYMR to depict the scene of a local railway station dating from 1922. Even those who have never visited it will have seen it, for it featured in the highly popular television series *Heartbeat* as Aidensfield and also as Hogsmeade in the *Harry Potter* films. Additionally, it provided a backdrop for *Brideshead Revisited* and *A Month in the Country*. Model railway enthusiasts may even own scale replicas of the footbridge, waiting room and platform which were included in the Skaledale Junction series produced by Hornby.

It is some 4 miles to the next station, and the line crosses the winding Eller Beck over four bridges. Around the third of these bridges once stood the short-lived Beckhole Station, opened in 1908. A small, tiled waiting shed alongside and not on the single platform formed a station where the service ended in 1914 with the outbreak of the First World War. It was never to reopen, although it was certainly still here until 1952, albeit overgrown and only used for its siding.

The Eller Beck is a tributary of the Murk Esk, joining to the west of the original line. The larger river is crossed via the Esk Valley Viaduct shortly before the original track – now the rail trail used by walkers – rejoins this line. Those

A diesel locomotive and rolling stock at Grosmont. (*Author*)

coming on foot will have the opportunity to view Grosmont Tunnel, a delightful piece of architecture built in 1836 as part of the horse-drawn railway of George Stephenson. Approaching by rail, it is impossible to appreciate the larger tunnel completed in 1847 alongside the original Grosmont Horse Tunnel.

The 1952-style Grosmont Station sits on old mine workings, iron ore being extracted until the North Eastern Railway owned the line. Today, the right to mine these seams belongs to the NYMR, although to do so would invite the danger of subsidence on a profitable line for little return.

From Grosmont we go across eight bridges, crossing the River Esk to reach Sleights, although there is no NYMR station here. The next stop is the terminus at Whitby some 7 miles away, before which we have to cross the Esk again, bypass Ruswarp railway station and travel along the side of the ever-widening river. Both line and river are crossed by the Larpool Viaduct, which once carried the Scarborough & Whitley Railway to meet the Whitby, Redcar & Middlesbrough Union Railway. Thirteen arches made of brick were designed by John Waddell, a Scottish-born railway contractor who also rebuilt Putney Bridge in London and played a large role in the construction of the Mersey Railway Tunnel. Today, the Grade II listed Larpool Viaduct carries a cycle path and footpath which is examined on the route to Scarborough.

The Esk itself is an important river for wildlife. Only 28 miles long but with little in the way of industry or large population centres, the water quality is most excellent. Salmon run the entire length, leaps having been provided to enable them to negotiate the weirs. It is tidal as far as Ruswarp, around Whitby it is famous for its sea trout, and higher up the freshwater pearl mussels are somewhat threatened by the build-up of silt. At one time the river valley was of great importance to local industry: coal was mined and, as we have already seen, iron ore and potash was extracted near Boulby – some of the tunnels ran out under the bed of the North Sea for distances of up to 6 miles.

Through Bog Hall Junction the line reaches its terminus at Whitby. No fewer than four lines once came to Whitby – one had already closed in 1958 by the time Dr Richard Beeching's report recommended the remaining three should also disappear. One was the other line to Scarborough, discussed in another chapter; the second we have just followed from Pickering; and the third has been evident for some time in the line to Middlesbrough. That this was the only survivor was largely down to the landscape, with tiny villages served by steep and narrow roads making bus travel impractical. Hence, effectively, schoolchildren demanded the Esk Valley line was saved rather than build the more logical double track to Pickering and on to York.

Incidentally, the line to Middlesbrough continued to Stockton-on-Tees and Thornaby Station. The gradient here proved difficult for locomotives, particularly in and around the tunnel where it was always very damp. Steam locomotives had sanding gear, but when British Rail retired steam and used diesel this was no longer fitted to the locomotives and the metal tyres on the diesels slipped on the metal rails, whereas sand had enabled the same tyres of the steam locomotives to gain a good grip.

Enough of Whitby's railway heritage survives to please the enthusiast, including the buildings and memorabilia at the museum. However, one thing which will not be found in the museum is now housed in the workshops of the NYMR: the machinery and skills required to make a lubricating device of such unparalleled simplicity and efficiency it requires virtually no maintenance other than an annual oil change and occasional top-up.

Two brothers were the proprietors of a century-old business in York and, with retirement approaching, they sought to locate their small workshop elsewhere. The NYMR seized the opportunity with both hands, seeing the chance to become the sole supplier of the Armstrong Oiler, which has lubricated bearings in rolling stock with an ingenious system. A spring steel frame is located on the axle box. Covering this is, of all things, a worsted cloth pad, itself provided with a continuous supply of clean oil by a pure cotton feeder, and thence to the bearing. These are made to order and sent to all four corners of the globe, including America, the Netherlands, South Africa, the Cook Islands, Trinidad, Sudan, Egypt, India, the Democratic Republic of the Congo, Kenya, and the Kowloon-Canton Railway in Hong Kong/China, which carries 1.5 million passengers over 22 miles of track every single day.

Inside Whitby Station it looks rather empty in 2012 …

... meanwhile, outside it has changed little in the twenty-first century. (*Author*)

The necessary talents and skills are drawn from individuals with experience gained at other railway locations and related industries. Many receive special training for important skills in-house, while particular attention is given to engineering, both mechanical and civil, and in the modern era safety is always an important consideration. These and other factors make the NYMR the only heritage line to be a registered Train Operating Company. Two of the individuals associated with the NYMR have received MBEs for their work. Undoubtedly the workforce, be they employees or volunteers, have every reason to be proud of their achievements thus far.

As with any business, there are long-term plans in place for the line with a number of targets set for the year 2020. Uppermost in their minds is an increase in the number of steam trains which can run to Whitby each day. Currently this is limited to three because Whitby was reduced to a basic terminus in the 1980s and remains so until the track and platforms are restored. But this is by no means all. Whitby Station is also planned to have a new platform, a run-around loop and dedicated steam railway station facilities. A new carriage shed at Pickering is also on the agenda, just a small part of a scheme which hopes to have all locomotives and rolling stock, be they on loan or owned by the line, undercover and in good working condition. This dovetails nicely with the training of future engineers, whose talents will bring in interest from elsewhere and create an invaluable resource for the future.

The North Yorkshire Moors Railway aims to be one of the great steam experiences, not only in the United Kingdom but in the world. It is certainly among the leaders of the pack.

10   SOUTH DEVON RAILWAY

This line has one claim to fame which no other can boast. Indeed, it seems likely few heritage lines would ever consider asking the infamous Dr Richard Beeching to reopen their line, especially just six years after the release of his even more infamous report. The tongue-in-cheek request was made by Terry Holder of *The Economist*, who came here to open the line on 21 May 1969.

Built as the Buckfastleigh, Totnes & South Devon Railway, it opened on 1 May 1872. Worked by the larger South Devon Railway Company, hence the present name, it was amalgamated into the Great Western Railway in two stages, firstly in 1876 and in its entirety in 1897. Aside from the nationalisation of the railways on 1 January 1948, little of significance happened until the closure of the line in September 1962. The line reopened in April 1969 as the Dart Valley Railway, a name which is still heard today, some twenty years after it was taken over by the South Devon Railway Trust and officially became the South Devon Railway.

Dr Richard Beeching opening the South Devon Railway at Buckfastleigh in 1969. (*Courtesy of John Brodribb*)

The line itself covers a little under 7 miles, much of it within sight of the upper reaches of the beautiful River Dart. Within easy reach of the present station at Totnes, which links with the line from London to Penzance, itself visible from Totnes Littlehempston Station, the current name of the South Devon Railway station previously known as Totnes Riverside. The 300yd walk between the two stations takes us across the river for the first time via a footbridge.

Totnes Littlehempston has but a single platform, with rolling stock in a bay siding featuring a small exhibit and a van containing memorabilia for sale. The booking office is a delight, a scene straight out of history. Staverton has one platform and is the only stop on the route aside from the termini. It closed to passenger traffic in 1958, although goods continued to be unloaded here for another four years.

Buckfastleigh has been the end of the line since the stretch to Ashburton was cut following improvements to the A38 trunk road in 1971. Again, there is only a single platform here, although sidings and indoor exhibits are on permanent show revealing something of the refurbishing work which goes on. Inside the shed is the locomotive *Tiny*, the sole remaining example of a broad gauge engine. The employees and volunteers here speak of the many ancillary tasks and services which are vital in ensuring visitors enjoy an authentic experience.

The large workshop at Buckfastleigh is where locomotives and rolling stock are repaired. In the twenty-first century spare parts are difficult to find; indeed many are impossible. Hence it is necessary to make these items from scratch and

This is all that remained of Buckfastleigh Station in 1964. (*Courtesy of Dr Ben Brooksbank*)

Buckfastleigh Station yard. (*Author*)

for Buckfastleigh, which has the capacity and employs the skills to produce the parts, this can be a real money-spinner. The workshops not only produce parts for their own needs, but also for other heritage sites around the country.

In order to maintain the high level of skills required to produce such parts, and also to maintain the locomotives and rolling stock, it is important to keep training and learning. Initially, the expertise came in the form of 'old boys' from the main line. Thereafter enthusiasts, all of whom had already displayed good engineering skills, were given the knowledge of the workings, nuances and tricks of the trade required in keeping a steam locomotive and its coaches on the rails.

One of the joys of travelling on many heritage railways is the tickets. No wispy pieces of printed computer paper here – the South Devon Railway still uses the old card tickets. A vital part of the heritage experience, these are purchased from the West Somerset Railway, while Edmondson tickets are purchased for the Santa Specials which run during advent.

Uniforms appear authentic, but on closer inspection they are ordinary jackets and trousers (not always a perfect colour match). Clearly over the years seamstresses have acquired a good collection of buttons and insignia which are sewn on to the 'new uniform' as the old one shows unacceptable signs of wear. There is no real dress code implemented, yet one cannot fail to be impressed by the personal standards set and met by those who wear them with pride.

The signs and advertisements, many of which are the distinctive and long-lasting variety painted on metal, have all been donated to the line. Only a few of these have required a touch-up of paint.

11   LLANGOLLEN RAILWAY

The Llangollen Railway, *Rheilffordd Llangollen* in Welsh, is by far the longest heritage railway line in the principality. At the time of writing, work was under way to extend the existing 7 miles to a total of 12.

Opened as the Ruabon to Llangollen line in 1862, it was extended through to the present station and to Corwen, connecting with the line to Barmouth, the first passenger traffic arriving here on 18 May 1865. It was then absorbed by the Great Western Railway in 1877. As a heritage line it was a slow starter: funding was scarce and progress was due to the generosity of others who offered materials, time and sponsorship. Donations from those who suffered from the cutbacks make the collection here of great interest. Among the engines are diesel locomotives, which are often overlooked in favour of steam yet have just as enthusiastic a following.

Originally the line ran off the Shrewsbury to Chester line, heading into Llangollen via stations at Acrefair and Trevor. Today, the line begins just below the Dee Bridge (as it is correctly known) at Llangollen, which was built in 1345 by Bishop Trevor of Trevor Hall. He could never have envisaged a railway station being named after him five centuries later. The Dee Bridge is a scheduled ancient monument and was largely unchanged until it was widened in the 1960s to meet the increasing demands of modern traffic.

The station at Llangollen stands alongside the River Dee, whose turbulent waters can be seen in the background. (*Author*)

When the railway came here in the nineteenth century, the population was centred towards the south-east. The remains of the early settlement still exists in the names of Church Street, Bridge Street and Green Lane, which ran close to the village green, but many of the residents were displaced by the coming of the railway. Earlier still, in 1815, the canal came through here and is still open for leisure cruises from Llangollen Wharf. You will need a head for heights, however, as it crosses the river via the aqueduct built by Thomas Telford, which at 126ft high is said to be the highest in the world. The importance of Llangollen as a major junction into Wales is clear: the canal, then the A5 trunk road to Holyhead, and finally the railway meant there were no fewer than three direct routes into London.

Two working signal boxes control traffic through the station up the gradient to and around Llangollen Goods Junction. Behind the scenes work is carried out at the engine shed and carriage workshop, with access to the main line. East of Llangollen, in 1945, the canal burst its banks and washed out the trackbed below. Sadly, the alarm was not raised quickly enough to prevent a mail train being derailed with the resulting death of the driver.

It is worthwhile noting that, following the closure of this line in January 1965, a bus service was supposed to offer alternative public transport. As with many of the bus routes, this was cut before long as there were insufficient passengers to make it pay. Customers would opt to buy a car, change jobs or even move house following the closure of the railway. This particular route is often cited as being the biggest loss-maker in Wales.

The following station is Berwyn, reached via the Berwyn Dee Bridge which proved a major obstacle in opening the line this far. Extensive work was required amounting to some £30,000, with loans and grants from the local council proving the only way to pay for it without many years of fundraising. The six masonry arches cross the point where a brook joins the Dee, while iron ribs support the site where the station platform itself sits. The Welsh Tourist Board, aware of the increased number of visitors the new line would bring, provided a grant to refurbish Berwyn Station. The first train to arrive here after the extension was in October 1985 and featured a diesel railcar, although the station had not been finished and it was not for another month that the first passenger could alight here.

A feature of the station which demands attention is the chain bridge which crosses the Dee to the Chain Bridge Hotel. At the time of writing it is closed and awaiting repair, however it is certainly one of the most photogenic points on the line.

Not only is this a heritage line, but the buildings have been utilised to the fullest extent. The old stationmaster's house at Berwyn has been refurbished delightfully to provide self-catering accommodation for a sizable family. Clearly intended to delight the railway enthusiast, guests are also treated to unlimited travel on the line during their stay.

The success of the extension inevitably led to calls for the line to continue. Leaving Berwyn across the viaduct, the line dives into the Berwyn Tunnel; at 689yd in length it is the longest single-bore tunnel in operation on a heritage line in Britain. It lacks smoke ventilation shafts, making the climb a difficult task for drivers who must ensure the engine does not stall, but it is lined with bricks throughout, a legacy of the ore mining (including lead) in the hill above. These old workings easily fill with water and leaks into the tunnel itself produce impressive icicles during cold spells.

Arriving at the request stop of Deeside Halt, take a look around to see what has been built entirely by volunteers. The platform, large enough for two coaches, was topped by a Great Western pagoda rescued from Ffestiniog Station and is used here as a waiting room. Volunteers were only able to watch as specialist engineers were called in to repair capping stones at tunnel portals.

Soon we come to Glyndyfrdwy Station, which not only had its track and signalling removed, but was demolished and grassed over and used as a children's playing field. Before work could begin, several trees which had become too big and were encroaching had to be removed. The signal box here came from Leaton and had been stored on the line for some time. A new level crossing was required and a new station building had to be built from scratch, as the original was now a private residence.

The first passenger-carrying trains since the Beeching Axe arrived here on 17 April 1992. Originally, the station was to have been closed on 18 January 1965;

Every station on the line has its own character; Glyndyfrdwy had acquired a collection of milk churns by the spring of 2011. (*Author*)

however, extensive flood damage was discovered on 14 December the previous year and no other train stopped here until the heritage line rebuilt the stop. It also provides a passing place on this busy line.

Passing Owain Glyndwr's Mount we arrive at the present terminus of Carrog. Again, flooding closed this station a few weeks prematurely, the trackbed and buildings were removed, with the signal box and waiting room on number two platform demolished as unsafe. This is also a passing place and has its own signal box. The station was reopened in 1996 by the Duke of Westminster, patron of the Llangollen Railway.

There are plans to extend the line through Bonwm Halt and on to Corwen, a distance of over 2 miles. This could potentially link it with the Ruabon to Barmouth line, which has been opened as a narrow gauge preservation line at Bala. A 10-mile section between Dolgellau and Barmouth is now a bridleway and cycle route known as the Mawddach Trail, or *Llwybr Mawddach* in Welsh, which will be explored under its own chapter.

12   GREAT CENTRAL RAILWAY

Few heritage sites can match the size and diversity of the Great Central Railway. And none can boast a dual track, for this is the only heritage line in Europe, and possibly the world, where locomotives in steam can be seen passing in opposite directions, just as they would have done in their heyday.

It could be argued that the modern version of the Great Central Railway qualifies as its heyday. As a heritage line it has already lasted longer than it ever did as part of British Rail or any of its earlier guises. Furthermore, returning to the subject of tracks, there are actually four around Swithland, with passing loops for both up and down lines.

In 1846 the Great Central Railway was created from three earlier companies: the Manchester, Sheffield and Lincolnshire. Eight years later, general manager Edward Watkin, who went on to become chairman in 1864, took steps to link the company to the busy industrial centres of Manchester and Sheffield. His vision for the future went further, linking this line to Europe via a proposed tunnel under the English Channel – an idea which finally reached fruition 130 years later.

In those days the many small railways were forced to negotiate with their rivals to use their lines and thereafter provide a connected service across the country. Watkin continually tried to browbeat the other companies into giving in to his demands, which would have been largely to his advantage. They united to thwart his plans and he was forced to build his own extension between Sheffield

Loughborough Station in December 1972. (*Courtesy of Dennis Wilcock*)

The opening of Quorn & Woodhouse Station on 24 June 1973. (*Courtesy of Dennis Wilcock*)

Quorn & Woodhouse Station. (*Author*)

and London. In 1899 this was finished and became the Great Central Railway; however, Watkin never saw the conclusion of his ambitious plans as ill health forced his retirement.

In 1923 the first great rationalisation of the nation's railway system brought this line under the control of the London & North Eastern Railway. Then, in 1948, it became part of British Rail as nationalisation took effect. This was the beginning of the end of the main line, for there was already an alternative line to run passenger and freight services. Long sections were closed in 1966 with the last part between Nottingham and Rugby finishing in 1969.

Almost immediately preservation enthusiasts stepped in, recognising the potential of this particular line. The first locomotive ran on the heritage line in 1973 and some thirty years later it was voted the twelfth best journey in the world on a list of fifty by railway enthusiasts. As a heritage line the company has provided opportunities for more than forty full-time staff and an army of more than 500 volunteers. Among the many factors which make it so popular must be the varied faces of the stations: Leicester North, for example, is not the original station – that was the Belgrave & Birstall Station. This is the only station not reached via steps from a bridge crossing the lines (although the original station was) – this can be seen from the remains of the entrance on the bridge in Station Road.

Loughborough appears as it did when it closed in the 1960s. What particularly dates the station are the headlines on the newspaper boards. People will remember

Looking over the bridge at Station Road, the former Belgrave & Birstall Station position is revealed by the tracks not being parallel. (*Author*)

The bricked-up entrance to what was the Belgrave & Birstall Station in Station Road. (*Author*)

A new engine shed under construction, 22 September 1974. (*Courtesy of Dennis Wilcock*)

The installation of the south points at Quorn & Woodhouse Station in December 1974.
(*Courtesy of Dennis Wilcock*)

the 1950s and 1960s through headlines such as 'Anthony Eden Resigns',
'Newcastle United Win the Cup' and 'Ruth Ellis Hangs for Murder'.

Loughborough's yard is long and busy, the variety of locomotives and rolling
stock quite striking compared to other heritage lines. Although numbers are
always changing, the skills of the workmen are renowned and other heritage
lines utilise their talents for repairs and restoration, so there are usually six steam
locomotives operational, with another three in various stages of restoration.
Another four are based here but are the property of the National Railway
Museum. Added to this, there are at least ten diesel locomotives located here.

North of Loughborough the lines end abruptly, with a break of some 100yd
in the embankment before it begins again and heads off towards Ruddington,
4 miles south of central Nottingham. The break had been swept away on the
orders of British Rail. In fact, the embankment still exists and has simply been
re-laid to allow trains to pass along here from the gypsum works at East Leake

A brake van at Quorn & Woodhouse Station, 23 June 1974. (*Courtesy of Dennis Wilcock*)

A patriotic scene at Rothley Station on 6 September 1975. (*Courtesy of Dennis Wilcock*)

Rothley signal box. (*Author*)

to connect to the Midland line. Not the busiest of lines, it carries no more than three trains a week.

One day the Great Central Railway hopes to reconnect the line to run all the way to Ruddington once more. This was the original idea and anyone who talks to the workers and volunteers will be convinced this is no mere dream and trains will run the 20 miles in each direction once more and make it one of the longest heritage lines in the land.

Quorn & Woodhouse Station recreates the period during the days of the Second World War. This may be because people come here to visit Beaumanor Hall nearby where, during the darkest days of the Second World War, some of the keenest minds on the planet met to help break the enemy's codes. While all the praise goes to Bletchley Park, other locations worked feverishly to break the most difficult of codes. Quorn & Woodhouse is rumoured to have played host to some of the most senior figures of the war.

Another link to the Second World War at Quorn & Woodhouse is its part in the D-Day landings. Although most people would never think that a quiet corner in the Leicestershire countryside could be the launching pad for American troops heading for France, there is good reason to believe US forces were loaded into coaches in the extensive yard here before heading for the south coast.

Rothley Station reflects the Edwardian era. On the platform are trucks loaded with period luggage with a background of suitable advertising. The attention to detail, particularly inside the station buildings, is epitomised by the plumbing and fittings in the gentlemen's facilities. And it is not only the inanimate that is seen at Rothley. There have long been reports of a ghostly figure here – an old signalman who is said to walk the platforms. However, a paranormal group recently investigated the station and found that the signalman is not alone. They reported a man in his fifties wearing a white shirt and braces. In the waiting room two Victorian ladies continue to wait: one is a young woman with a parasol; the second is a more mature woman seated in the chair by the door. A party of schoolboys with their teacher standing on the platform has also been witnessed.

An impressive collection of locomotives can be found at Loughborough. Some steam ...

... and others diesel. (*Author*)

None of the themes at any of the stations were actually planned: the Edwardian era, the Second World War and the days of the closure of the line in the 1960s simply sprung up as backdrops. Indeed, it is likely these 'themes' were created out of the memorabilia that was available. As a result, these differences have enabled the line to be used as the setting for several film and television productions. *Shadowlands* with Sir Anthony Hopkins, *The Hours* with Nicole Kidman and the 2001 hit movie *Enigma* all saw the stations on the Great Central Railway being filmed as Oxford, Manchester Piccadilly and Bletchley.

Television has also brought cameras here. The Ricky Gervais-directed *Cemetery Junction* was filmed here, as was an episode of *Casualty* and a mystery solved by Miss Marple. In addition, the *Top Gear* team camped here for two weeks while a car and several caravans were modified to run on rails rather than roads. Novelists have also used the line as inspiration for their works. At least three novels have been set in this area, including Stephen Done's *Marylebone Murders*.

During the year a number of re-enactment days are scheduled. The Second World War re-enactment group travel here to add their own particular flavour to the day. While the men play soldiers and drive the old model trucks and cars, the women attend to every detail and wield a needle and thread to make the all-important changes to clothing; and the period hairstyles are works of art. Of course, the highlight for all is to ride on the train. During the 1950s, when the English holiday resorts enjoyed their greatest success, the journey was as much a part of the holiday as the beach.

For those who used the train regularly, the quality of the food served in the dining car was unquestioned. At the Great Central Railway this dining experience attracts great numbers; but spare a thought for those who cook and serve your meal. While diners can see the skills of the waiters, behind the scenes two or three chefs work in the most cramped conditions, preparing sumptuous dishes using the original kitchens and equipment of the dining cars. Chefs have no room to swing the proverbial cat and waiters perform balancing acts more suited to the circus than the railway.

Whatever the future holds for the Great Central Railway, we can be sure the staff will go forward with a smile and a desire to succeed.

13   THE WHISKY LINE

The Keith & Dufftown Railway was built by the company of this name formed in 1857, the line opening five years later. Not a decade later, in 1866, it was absorbed into the Great North of Scotland Railway. It remained independent until the nationalisation of the railway network in 1948.

Today it is a heritage railway and affectionately known as the Whisky line because it links the market town of Keith with Dufftown, said to be the malt whisky capital of the world – and with no fewer than seven working distilleries, few can have a better claim. It is unusual for a heritage railway because it has no steam, only diesel locomotives. Also, the buildings which form the stations, signal boxes, engine houses etc. are all originals, albeit once derelict.

Dufftown, a town founded by the Earl of Fife in 1817 as the ideal place for a distillery owing to the quality of its water, produces the famed Glenfiddich whisky. This is the only Highland single malt to be distilled, matured and bottled on one site – that site being next to the railway station where the fifth generation of the Grant family invite visitors to view the process and sample the finished product.

A short branch of the Speyside Way links Dufftown to Craigellachie. Over 40 miles of this long-distance footpath, mainly on the former trackbeds of the Great North of Scotland Railway, links Spey Bay to Tomintoul near Grantown-on-Spey and the Strathspey Railway.

As the train pulls out of Dufftown it passes the railway yard, offering good views of the rolling stock before passing the walls of Balvenie Castle and crossing Fiddich Viaduct. There follows a steep gradient of 1 in 60 reaching 590ft above sea level. Here are the sources of both the River Isla and the tributaries of the Fiddich.

The next stop is a halt. Loch Park serves the man-made loch in the narrow valley at the head of the Isla. The adventure centre here offers many outdoor pursuits: canoeing, kayaking, camping, assault courses, orienteering, mountain biking, and numerous walks of which some are suitable for wheelchair users.

Further along the line keep an eye out for Drummuir Castle, overlooking Drummuir Station in its sheltered wooded valley. At the time of writing only one of the original two platforms has been restored, although future plans include the second platform, a passing loop and a locomotive shed.

While the platform at Towiemore Halt has crumbled away over the years, the shelter is still intact and used as a store – it was also originally intended to be used as a shelter by volunteers in the winter months. There was once a waiting room here made from the body of an old Great North of Scotland Railway coach. Look to the left and the warehousing occupies the old goods yard and was where volunteers cleared the vegetation, leading to the discovery of the original gates.

Leaving Towiemore the line bends to the left, coming out of the pine forest into farmland, and runs alongside the Isla before swinging left again and into Auchindachy. The old station is still here but is now a private house and the platform this side has gone. Over the line the other platform still serves passengers who may be visitors to the Victorian watermill, still complete with waterwheel but not in working order. Plans to develop the mill as a restaurant have been shelved, although they could well be revived in the future as the line continues to be improved. First, the drainage problem would have to be overcome, as the station area lies very close to the river and a tributary. The proximity of the river is obvious as we leave Auchindachy and the line crosses it twice.

Descending into Keith, there is another distillery on the left and the Strathmill siding is nearby. Keith Station stands below the main road in a deep cutting, making it seem isolated from the platform. Today's station is only 10 years old but it is based on the long-gone original which was a split-level station. Keith boasts one of the oldest packhorse bridges in Scotland, known as Auld Brig and built in 1609. The distillery is the oldest in this part of Scotland, dating from 1768, yet the waters were used in brewing at least 500 years before the first dram of whisky was produced.

Although trains travel no further, the line does not end here. Down the half-a-mile gradient of 1 in 70 we find Keith Junction Station. Here, the line is able to connect with the main line, although there are buffers and part of the track has been lifted at the insistence of Railtrack (the company responsible for maintaining the track and trackbed at the time). Two of the four original platforms have been removed, but the sidings from the main track remain and reconnection to the main line for rail tours sometime in the future seems inevitable, especially as the *Royal Scotsman* is already located here as the luxury train part of the package for short holiday cruises.

Travel along this line and you will realise that it is one of the most scenic routes in the country. With plenty of scope for development, this is clearly a work in progress and visitor numbers will undoubtedly increase.

14 COLNE VALLEY RAILWAY

Despite being one of the shortest heritage lines in Britain, at only a mile in length, it is certainly worthy of inclusion. Opened as the Colne Valley & Halstead Railway over a three-year period from April 1860, it formed part of the line from Birdbrook to Wakes Colne. The service ran virtually unchanged for a century until the last passenger train came through on 30 December 1961. Freight traffic continued for another four years, with the line lifted and buildings demolished in 1966 as a result of the Beeching Report.

Winding forward seven years, the land was purchased by the Colne Valley Railway and in 1974 their first locomotive arrived, closely followed by a second. Soon after, the preservation society were running these locomotives along a short section of track and attracting great public interest, despite there being no infrastructure whatsoever. Hedingham Station was still standing but located a mile away. Hence, planning permission was sought and granted; the building was purchased; and detailed plans were put in place to rebuild the station. Painstakingly taken down brick by brick, with each piece carefully numbered to ensure it was replaced in exactly the same position, Hedingham Station was rebuilt and became the first permanent construction on the heritage line.

The same could not be done with the signal box, for this had been destroyed long ago. A suitable replacement was found at Cressing on the Braintree branch line. Again, the building was transported to Hedingham, where the timber box was mounted on a lower tier of newly laid brickwork to raise it even higher than the original. The rail bridge has always crossed the River Colne, although not here but at nearby Earls Colne further along its course.

Plans are in force to extend the line further, doubling its length to some 2 miles. The route has been cleared and is now open for walkers and cyclists to Yeldham. However, before the trains can run again there would have to be inspections of the route, which is rather narrow in places, and renovations of the platforms.

15   GWILI RAILWAY

The Gwili Railway, *Rheilffordd Gwili* in Welsh, is the name of the heritage line which began as the Carmarthen & Cardigan Railway. When it opened in 1860 the line was operating at the original broad gauge of 7ft ¼in. Twenty years later it became part of the Great Western Railway, solving its ongoing financial problems at a stroke.

The Manchester & Milford Railway joined this line at Pencader, which eventually brought the line to Lampeter and Aberystwyth. Shortly afterwards, in 1872, the line changed to the standard 4ft 8½in now used everywhere. This made it the last in Wales to use Brunel's wider gauge. During the Second World War this line carried heavy ammunition between North and South Wales, but at other times the line was the epitome of the scenic Welsh branch line, meandering at no great speed through farmland. Indeed, the 56-mile journey between Carmarthen and Aberystwyth took three hours, not helped by the new halts. These official request stops were not the only places these trains stopped, however: farmers' wives on the way to market would hail the train to stop from the fields!

Minor branches to Aberaeron and Newcastle Emlyn closed in 1952, although the Butlins camp at Pwllheli provided a brief boost to passenger numbers. The Beeching Report did recommend closure, though, and the last passenger service ran in February 1965 with the final freight delivery made in 1973. It was to be a further five years before the heritage line saw the light of day, even though the Gwili Railway Company had been formed three years earlier when all but a mile of the track had been lifted. Thus, while 8 miles had been earmarked for preservation, between Abergwili Junction and Llanpumsaint, only 1 mile of track remained, north from Bronwydd Arms.

Since those early days the line has been extended 2½ miles to Dan-y-Coed, with plans to restore the next leg as far as Carmarthen. While the collection of locomotives and rolling stock continues to grow, work on Bronwydd Arms Station has continued to produce a replica Great Western Railway station dominated by the signal box. This is a remarkably well-preserved piece of railway history constructed in 1885 and continues to operate the signalling on the current line.

This is, of course, Wales and looking around it is impossible not to see the hills and mountains which proved a headache to the original railway builders. Therefore, the line has sharp twists and turns, meandering around to avoid massive engineering work in the form of viaducts, bridges and tunnelling. It naturally follows the A484 road which, in turn, largely mirrors the River Gwili, which gave the line its name.

Gradients are inevitable, however, and there are some notable inclines. The first is seen in the 1 in 60 immediately north of Bronwydd Arms, with the line continuing to climb to the station at Penybont. A refurbished bridge carries the line across the River Gwili and to the station at Llwyfan Cerrig. The English name would be Stone Platform, derived from it once being a quarryman's halt. The quarry itself has long been closed and nature has been encouraged to return along the artery formed by the river in the form of a nature trail. It could be argued that cutting the railway ensured the quarry was no longer worked and a vital habitat was returned to the native species of the Welsh countryside; thus, the Beeching Report may have contributed to saving some of the endangered flora and fauna of our lands. The preservation line has encouraged visitors to enjoy the sights and sounds to be found here: a path leads from the platform to a picnic area; a miniature railway attraction has been set up; and treasure hunts are organised during school holidays and bank holidays.

Climbing on, the line runs along a shelf of land with the river on the left and the hewn rock face to the right. Three-quarters of a mile from the last station we arrive at Dan-y-Coed, a name meaning 'the foot of the wood', where a typical rural halt has been constructed which faithfully recreates the days when the Great Western Railway ran through.

While the line is currently set up to run just one engine at a time, there are passing loops for busy theme weekends. This has meant speciality events have been offered to fill the diary at quiet times, including Dining on Rails, Jazz Nights and, of course, Driving Experience. Hence, the boom in preservation railways has given Joe Public the opportunity to fulfil what was once many a schoolboy's dream: to drive a railway engine.

To continue further north becomes increasingly difficult, for the volunteers have another seven bridges to overcome before they reach the desired terminus of Llanpumsaint. All seven are in need of much repair – expensive work requiring specialist knowledge and skills. However, the trackbed to the south is also available to the society as far as Abergwili Junction, 2 miles south of Bronwydd Arms. In 2007 the Swansea Vale Railway closed and, while the future of that railway is still undecided, it has provided the Gwili Railway with track materials, a footbridge, water tanks, cranes and signalling equipment, etc. – all of which are ideal resources for the southern extension. Unfortunately, the work cannot start until funding and permission has been obtained for the access road to the new station at Abergwili Junction.

16   BO'NESS & KINNEIL RAILWAY

The Beeching cuts certainly affected Scotland as much as they did England and Wales; indeed, some 300 stations were closed. Yet it cannot correctly be said that any of the current heritage railways north of the border were saved or reopened after the closures.

In the case of the Bo'ness & Kinneil line, these 5 miles of track are operated by the Scottish Railway Preservation Society, while Bo'ness Station will become the site of the planned Scottish Railway Museum. The collection of engines (both steam and diesel) and rolling stock is greater than any preservation in Scotland.

There are four stops on the line, beginning with the terminus of Bo'ness. This is not the original station – that was a quarter of a mile away and is now buried beneath the concrete of a car park. The present station buildings are not those from the original station but have been rescued from demolition at other sites. Of the booking office, footbridge, bay platform and train shed, the latter is the most important from a historical perspective. Not only are such items rarely seen today, but this example came from Edinburgh Haymarket Station, the terminus of the Edinburgh & Glasgow Railway. It is a real piece of history, with its cast-iron columns and arched spans, and it is a listed building.

The station office building was saved from the North British Railway at Wormit on the shores of the Tay, near the Tay Bridge opposite Dundee. What was Garnqueen South Junction signal box is now at Bo'ness, taken from the former Caledonian Railway line, while further along the Highland Railway and north of Perth once stood Murthly Station; this station provided the footbridge for Bo'ness Station. Collectively, this group of buildings has been listed as Category A by Historic Scotland, while the cafe and tourist information occupy a modern building.

The current developments as the base for the Scottish Railway Preservation Society means a sizable area devoted to storing, maintaining and restoring a good number of locomotives and rolling stock. Furthermore, this area is being opened to viewing by the public, including access for the disabled.

Being named the Bo'ness & Kinneil Railway, perhaps we would expect to find something more substantial at Kinneil. However, it is not the request stop here which gave its name to the railway, nor is it the present Kinneil nature reserve; it is the former Kinneil Colliery which resulted in the request stop. This was the original terminus for the heritage railway. When serving the colliery the line was constructed with some tight curves. With the present line using these curves it is limited to 10mph through this section, which does have the advantage of allowing views of the reserve, developed on what was previously a scar on the countryside created by the mining operations.

In 1989 an extension was opened to Birkhill, a town best known for the Birkhill Fireclay Mine which is alongside the station. As at Bo'ness, none of the station buildings are original. However, here, unlike Bo'ness, they all came from one place – the Monifieth Railway Station – and were transferred here after being originally rebuilt for the 1988 Glasgow Garden Festival.

The station building today serves as the entrance to the fireclay mine. When the mine was still open there was no Birkhill Station, merely a siding, a loop and a water column. When the station was situated here it required the gradient to be lowered and a passing loop to be created. Reducing the height at Birkhill may seem a little excessive – why not simply utilise the former trackbed? Firstly, it made the station double as the entry to the mine, but also, and more importantly, it made the planned link to Manuel Junction possible.

Recently, the success of the line has enabled trains to be comprised of seven coaches, with the platform being extended accordingly. Currently in the planning stage is a signal box, built in the Caledonian style to fit in with that at Bo'ness and containing as many as twenty levers.

Trains first ran to Manuel Junction in 2010 and it links to the main line running from Glasgow to Edinburgh via Falkirk. The track was lifted in 1967 with the closure of the upper station, the lower level having shut its doors thirty-four years earlier. At present, Manuel does not have a station, but the connection to the main line does allow rail tours to connect directly on to this heritage line. It also enables the locomotives and rolling stock for the Scottish Railway Museum to be brought by rail, which is much easier and cheaper than transferring them by road.

17   LAKESIDE & HAVERTHWAITE RAILWAY

Surprisingly, this railway is one of the few surviving Beeching closures in the north-west of England. This former branch line of the Furness Railway was opened as a heritage line in 1973.

Originally opened in June 1859, the branch came off the Carnforth to Barrow-in-Furness main line at Ulverston and headed east through the junction at Plumpton, then serving Haverthwaite, Newby Bridge and Lakeside. Advertised as a connection with boat excursions, by 1922 eight trains were travelling in each direction every day. During the summer months specials from Lancashire and further afield were commonplace. Arriving at Lakeside passengers made the short hop to the boats sailing on Lake Windermere.

The lure of a combined train and boat trip to the lakes waned and by the time the Beeching Report was published in 1963, passenger numbers had declined markedly. Hence, the last British Rail passenger came through here in September 1965, with freight running for two more years.

Almost immediately enthusiasts formed the Lakeside Railway Estates Company with the aim of preserving both line and locomotive and eventually running steam trains. A new Labour government led by Harold Wilson, with Barbara Castle as Transport Minister, backed the idea. Yet in an unexpected twist the project failed when it was revealed that bridges would be required where the line crossed the trunk roads.

Nevertheless, through the drive and leadership of Dr Peter Beet, a visitor attraction known as Steamtown was built at Carnforth. The centrepiece was Dr Beet's LMS Class 10A locomotive already held there. The venture lasted some twenty years until taken over by businessman David Smith, who brought his own ideas in the form of the West Coast Railway Company. Meanwhile, a somewhat truncated version of the line was opened by the chairman Austin Maher in May 1973. On these 3½ miles Maher and fellow director Jim Morris ran their own LMS 2-6-4T Class 4MT locomotives, Nos 42073 and 42085.

Today, the line boasts nine steam locomotives and seven diesel locomotives, about half of which are operational and the remainder are in various stages of repair and/or restoration. The main station is at Lakeside, where it still connects to boat trips on Windermere and also offers access to the visitor attraction known as the Aquarium of the Lakes. At the time of closure in 1965, the station had two platforms and a roof, but British Rail undertook the removal of the roof and demolished one platform and the clock tower in 1978. The steamboat ferry service, which they had inherited as part of the line when the railways were nationalised in 1948, was sold off to a private concern.

The middle stop on this fifteen-minute journey is at Newby Bridge. While closed by British Rail in 1965, services were withdrawn much earlier. Indeed, until the heritage line reopened Newby Bridge as an unstaffed halt in 1973, no train had stopped here since 1939. A plaque shows the commemorative tree planted by Bishop Eric Treacy at the reopening ceremony.

The smaller terminus is Haverthwaite, with a sidings and goods shed. One long siding served the ironworks blast furnace at Backbarrow, and as recently as 1935 gunpowder produced at the local mills was brought here along a horse-drawn narrow gauge tramway. As with Newby Bridge, services ended here well before the line's official closure in 1965. The station shut its doors in 1955, although the last passenger service left much earlier in September 1946.

Today, the large station building, housing a booking hall and waiting room, is the major building alongside toilets, a sizable outside seating area, a footbridge and a second platform, although the latter two are not in use. More engine sheds and workshops are found here, and it is still possible to extend the line as far as Greenodd, although this would require a level crossing.

While this is one of the shortest heritage lines it is certainly among the most scenic and the future of the railway is looking promising.

18　AMBERGATE TO PYE BRIDGE

Running through Derbyshire this line has a unique claim to fame. It was a Beeching closure – the route closed on 23 December 1968 – however, no passenger service had run along here since June 1947. While the line closed by virtue of the recommendations of the report, British Rail did not take over the railways until 1948, so this railway has never officially carried a BR passenger.

The line was intended to link the Midland main line with the Erewash Valley line and opened first to freight and then to passengers in 1875. This enabled coal from the Nottinghamshire coalfields to find its way to Manchester and Liverpool without going to Derby. Since closure, some of the track has been preserved, while another section is now occupied by a road.

Formerly, the Ambergate end of the line was a junction between this route and the line between Belper and Matlock. It is part of the London to Manchester route and now part of the Monsal Trail, dealt with in the next chapter. The buildings were removed in 1970, the road bridges twenty years later. There is still a station here – on the single track to Matlock which was the original main line between Derby and Sheffield via Chesterfield. Currently, an hourly service operates between Nottingham and Matlock. In recent years passenger numbers have increased significantly, with some 40,000 now seen annually.

Originally, Bullbridge was the next point on the line. Now a hamlet with two pubs, it was once just a bridge taking the road from Crich over the River Amber. This village would probably never have existed had it not been for two modes of transport coming through: first the canal and later the railway, both serving the Crich Quarry. Subsidence in the Butterley Tunnel has now closed the canal, the railway was closed by the report, and the quarry site is now derelict.

Reaching Hammersmith we find the first sign of the heritage line. Although this is the terminus, this station exists solely for those crossing the causeway over Butterley Reservoir. Other than the platform there is a signal box, which was built in 1900 at Kilby Bridge in Leicestershire and brought here in 1986. Trains also use the loop to run the engine around before the return journey. A possible extension to the west below the A38 and perhaps as far as Sawmills has been suggested, but nothing has been done to raise the necessary finances.

It is but a short distance to Butterley. Closed in 1964, the station was demolished shortly after the lifting of the line in 1968. Thirteen years later, the Midland Railway Trust reopened the station. Volunteers brought a station from Whitwell and reassembled it at Butterley. With the addition of a signal box from Ais Gill (on the Settle to Carlisle line) and the rebuilding of one of the two original platforms, the station was reopened on 22 August 1981.

Next we come to Swannick, the last station on the heritage line but not the end of the journey. In British Rail days this was a junction only; no station existed here until the heritage days. All the buildings have been brought here: the station building, for example, comes from Syston in Leicestershire; an old signal box from sidings at Desford Colliery has been utilised as office space; while the box from Kettering in Northamptonshire houses the working frame.

There are four platforms here today, although only number two is used by passengers. Platform one allows access to coaches, some of which have been converted into shops. Numbers three and four are an island platform and plans are well advanced to run diesel shuttles along the branch line to the former Swanwick Colliery. Although there is no access to this island platform at the time of writing, there is a footbridge, but disabled access has yet to be installed.

Belper Station prior to closure. (*Courtesy of Dr Ben Brooksbank*)

The station at Belper in 2011. (*Author*)

When trains are operating they only stop when heading westward; those travelling east pass straight through this short stretch running on to Riddings and Ironville. There are no platforms at either of these two locations at present, but there are plans to extend the 3½ miles to include stops at both places. Indeed, the heritage line hopes to run as far as the Erewash Valley line, where a junction with the main line and its train services would prove invaluable for bringing in more passengers.

While the line is currently quite short, scope for extending it and carrying more passengers is well within its capabilities. Not only is the trackbed still available, but in terms of locomotives and rolling stock the line is certainly blessed. Already these enable the line to run a series of themed events each year, including Thomas the Tank Engine weekends.

The Midland Railway has cleverly marketed the station buildings as museum pieces, which bring in their own enthusiasts. Also, there are a number of model railways for those who are interested. There are two OO gauge layouts at Butterley, with a 16MM layout in the gardens. Another two OO gauge layouts are at Swanwick with a larger N gauge layout also on view. The company boasts a light gauge line at Swanwick and a miniature line at Butterley, both of which are capable of carrying passengers.

Most of the locomotives are owned by others, be they individuals or interested bodies, and are permanently stationed here alongside those of the Midland Railway Trust. Currently, there are some twenty steam engines associated with the line: half on display, the remainder working or undergoing overhaul. When it comes to the forty diesel engines, fifteen are operational and a similar number are undergoing or awaiting repair or restoration.

Added to this are fourteen diesel multiple units and electric multiple units, eighteen suitable for running on the light railway, and another three on the miniature line. All these are used to pull more than sixty coaches. Clearly this is one line where the future is looking very bright indeed.

One of the many themed weekends at the Midland Railway. Here, the Railway Modellers were invited to see two much larger locomotives than those they were normally associated with. (*Courtesy of the Midland Railway Trust Ltd*)

PART III
PATHS & PRESERVATIONS

19   MONSAL TRAIL

This trail runs a little under 9 miles through the Peak District, and now that the tunnels have been reopened, it is one of the delights afforded by the Beeching Report. Prior to this, detours around the tunnels meant it was not possible to emerge from the tunnel on to the magnificent viaduct. This opened in 2012 at a cost of £3.785 million, making it equally accessible to walkers and cyclists.

This is a section of the route between Manchester and Matlock, which was opened in 1863 and closed in 1968. Twelve years without use was followed by the site coming under the control of the Peak District National Park. The present trail begins at Topley Pike near Buxton and follows the course of the River Wye and A6 trunk road to Coombs Viaduct near Bakewell.

The major landmarks on this largely flat trail, aside from the tunnels, are the viaducts which offer some of the most splendid views anywhere in the Peak District. The first encountered is at Miller's Dale, where the original 1866 version was joined by a second built parallel to the first in 1905, making four tracks. Following the tunnel we come to the railway station of Miller's Dale, which as a junction connected travellers on the London and Manchester line with Buxton.

With the next tunnel reopened it means the route ignores Litton Mill, which was founded in 1782 by Ellis Needham and Thomas Frith, farmers with small estates locally. Unlike other mills the locals had no weaving traditions; these sparsely populated areas were the abode of farmers who had neither knowledge nor interest in cotton. Their business was doomed to fail: no trained workforce, no buyer, a depression in the industry, fires and manufacturing problems – the list is endless. Both men barely scraped together a living and opted to take pauper children into their employ by means of an indenture sworn before a Justice of the Peace. Through this they undertook to provide for the child in terms of food and lodging, as well as employment. Essentially this was an excellent system; however, it tended to attract those looking for cheap labour and also relieved the parish of their responsibility. It was inevitable that it would prove corrupt. Both men were eventually declared bankrupt.

Negotiating another tunnel once closed for reasons of safety, we pass Cressbrook. This village did not exist as such until the textile mills were constructed here by Richard Arkwright, then later J.L. Phillips and Henry McConnell, who also took it upon himself to build the model village from around 1840 to house the workforce. The village remained a private estate until 1965, when the mill closed and the buildings were sold off to the public.

Within a few hundred yards we come to Monsal Dale. This is the most famous part of the route for the land around provides views over the viaduct and its valley from Monsal Head. Today, the Headstone Viaduct, as it should be called, is the focal point, yet this was not always the case. At 300ft in length and 40ft maximum height, the five 50ft arches were considered an eyesore when first constructed. In 1970, now without the railway tracks, this 'eyesore' was protected by a preservation order.

Skirting Great Longstone and Little Longstone we arrive at Hassop, a village that grew around its lead mines, which were given names such as Harry Bruce, Brightside, Waterhole and Whitecoe. The station is over a mile away, and today a cafe and bookshop occupy the station building.

The line passes through Bakewell, famous for its pudding, which no fewer than three local shops claim to have created. Note this is not the Bakewell 'tart', which is produced by commercial bakeries; this is a pudding consisting of a jam pastry, with a filling that includes an egg and ground almonds.

Today, the platform at the former Hassop Station makes a good seat and the trackbed the perfect cycle path with its gentle gradients. (*Author*)

A mile south of Bakewell we come to Coombs Viaduct, and shortly afterwards the Haddon Tunnel comes into view. Created to contain the trains it is often a surprise to hear the roof is only 11ft below ground level. This 'tunnel' was created by the same method as the early London Underground tunnels: cut into the ground to the required depth, with a man-made roof and covered with some of the spoil. This method was used instead of a simple cutting because the line runs through the Haddon Hall estate, and the Duke of Rutland insisted that if the line must come through his land, his view was not to be spoiled by the passage of steam locomotives.

The construction of this length of tunnel did not come without a price. On 2 July 1861 the tunnel collapsed and five men lost their lives. As the memorial stone tells us, James Birds of Youlgreave aged 43 years; James Millington of Stanton aged 45 years; Alfred Plank of Rowsley aged 16 years; George Buckley of Matlock aged 36 years; and James Clarke of Leicester aged 21 years lost their lives that day.

From Rowsley it is a short distance to the Peak Rail heritage line. It has been proposed that trains should be run again as far as Bakewell, but this has yet to meet with approval and, at the time of writing, no timetable has been set out.

20   TARKA TRAIL

The Tarka Trail is a footpath and cycle path which runs in a figure-of-eight route around England's scenic county of Devon. Not every one of these 180 miles runs along a former railway line and not all of this route where a railway line once existed was closed by Beeching.

It forms part of the Devon Coast to Coast Cycle Route, linking Ilfracombe in the north with Plymouth in the south. It is designated National Cycle Network Route 27, 102 miles of which are largely former railway lines, including the Ilfracombe branch line, Bideford Extension Railway, and the North Devon Railway.

The origin of the Tarka Trail is comparatively recent. Purchased for £500,000 in 1986, the disused railway line between Barnstaple and Bideford became part of the Taw/Torridge Country Park the following year. So successful did this venture prove that in 1989 Devon County Council purchased the rest of the line from Bideford to Meeth. The expense of the extension did not put any initial strain on the budget because the invoice totalled just 100 pence. Grants enabled this new section to be completed and most of the £160,000 was used to pay for the adaptation and repair of the bridges across the River Torridge.

Contributions by the local authorities, parish councils and National Trust were vital in ensuring that the numerous access points, parking and refreshment stops were made available along the route. These bodies also ensured minimum

The railway station at Barnstaple ...

disturbance to the environment, even to the point of bringing in the Otter Conservation Officer to make sure there was no disruption to the mammal which gave this project its name, taken from the book *Tarka the Otter* by Henry Williamson. Not until 1997 was the route fully open to Meeth – a quarry having been opened across the line since the railway closed.

There are reminders of Williamson's books all along the trail. Marker stones, shaped and brightly coloured, include quotes from the characters of the author's most famous book. Indeed, at Braunton, bicycles are available at Otter Cycle Hire.

Beginning in the north at the former Ilfracombe Station, there are clear reminders of a working station. For those interested, the local museum holds several items from the station and the array of photographs provides an interesting viewpoint, seeing the 'before' prior to travelling the 'after'. As a popular holiday destination the trains arriving on summer Saturdays were necessarily lengthy and required the extensive sidings as stabling prior to the return journey. Ilfracombe Station also boasted two platforms, an engine shed, turntable, and a sizable goods yard now occupied by a factory.

... is also home to Tarka Trail Cycle Hire. (*Author*)

While the official cycle route begins at the harbour, we shall begin at the station itself, aptly found on Station Road towards the south-west of the town. Leaving via the path which takes us around the factory, we climb slowly through the double-bore tunnels and past the scenic Slade Reservoirs. Thereafter, the trackbed swings west towards Borough Cross where these paths fork. In order to follow the Ilfracombe branch line faithfully, we should take the right-hand track, leading north-west to Mortehoe.

Correctly, the station was known as Mortehoe & Woolacombe, the name of the sands stretching along the North Devon coast. This station lay derelict for many years until, in 1990, it became the basis for a children's theme park called Once Upon A Time. This most unique park owed its very existence to the Beeching closures. Following the purchase of the station, four British Rail Mark I coaches were also acquired and refurbished to show animated fairy tales to complement the rides found in and around the station buildings. The track had vanished twenty years previously and thus a crane had to be hired to drop all four into the station between the platforms.

The attraction closed in 2005 when the land was sold to a developer. However, this small holiday village was designed to complement the appearance of the railway station, with the signal box being used as a reception area and the new houses built from brick and tile reminiscent of the old railway buildings.

The 15 miles from Ilfracombe was the longest leg of the journey. The next section, of just 6 miles, brings us to the town of Barnstaple. The route largely follows the coast, past Woolacombe Sands, turning inland again through Putsborough and Georgeham, before turning south and entering Braunton. At Braunton there is evidence of the former railway in several places. Oddly, the first evidence is on the road, or perhaps we should say in the road, for here the rails are still embedded in the tarmac at the old level crossing over the B3231. In Braunton itself the station is still standing, currently serving as the local newsagents; but easily recognisable is the goods shed, which doubles as the local youth club. There is no problem finding the original station as the old street name of Station Road survives, also inspiring the recent development of Signal Court.

South of Braunton the line crossed a second level crossing before reaching the small station at Wrafton. Here, the single platform and two goods sidings served the village and the local station at RAF Chivenor. The station is now a private building, the siding houses camping coaches, and the military base has been home to the Royal Marines since 1998.

Shortly afterwards we enter the largest town on our route: Barnstaple. This section to Barnstaple was featured in the BBC series *James May's Toy Stories*, when May attempted to run a model train along the old 4ft 8½in standard gauge railway route. The station is now closed, although until recent years the signal box was used as a museum.

Fremington Quay is the next point, a distance of some 2 miles. The village of Fremington is best known for Fishley Pottery, although the clay pits are long worked out. Similarly, the busy quayside no longer has its trains or its steam cranes used to load and unload goods arriving by both rail and sea.

Today, the track crosses Fremington Pill by way of the old London & South Western Railway iron bridge – *pill* is an Old English or Saxon word describing a tidal river. Visitors may think the Quay Cafe is a remnant from Beeching's closures, but despite its appearance it is no old railway building; rather a recent building made to look like an original. The old station buildings were on the opposite side of the trail and the old platform is still visible.

Another 4 miles along is Instow, overlooking the expansive sands of Instow Beach and the River Torridge beyond. Instow's railway station saw its last passenger in 1965, although freight continued until 1982 carrying ball clay. The most notable remnant of the old railway station is the signal box, now over 130 years old and the first building of its kind in the land to be given a Grade II listing. When in operation it controlled the signals and level crossing south of the station.

The levers still work as well as ever, with one operating a signal here, and the wheel to open and close the crossing gates is also evident. For those with an interest, the signal box is managed by volunteers and is open to visitors on Sundays and public holidays. The volunteers offer tuition on the workings of the signals and in return ask for a donation towards the upkeep of the box.

From Instow it is only 3 miles to Bideford, the route taking us alongside the east bank of the River Torridge and affording some of the best views in this part of Devon. With the main body of the town on the opposite shore, there was

The track is still visible, embedded in the road at the former level crossing over the B3231 in Braunton. (*Author*)

plenty of room for the railway and Bideford Station. Although there have been no passenger trains since 1965, there were plans to reopen the station and relay part of the line as a heritage railway. It is clear that much work had already been completed when the project came to an abrupt halt in 2008 and the future of Bideford Station is once again uncertain.

The trail comes south to cross the Torridge near Landcross. Here, the river had been canalised to allow vessels to travel up to the lime kilns at Annery and Weare Giffard. There is a record of a visit in 1971 to the eighteenth-century cottages associated with the kilns when one of the chimneys was found to be alight. Calmly the tenant took out his gun and fired both barrels of his twelve-bore shotgun up the chimney, thus 'extinguishing the fire and cleaning the chimney at the same time'.

Shortly afterwards we pass Beam House, a private residence whose name was shared by the aqueduct which has been used as a road bridge for many years. Some may recognise the bridge for it provided the backdrop to many scenes in the film version of *Tarka the Otter*.

Great Torrington is a distance of 5 miles from Bideford. Built for the London & South Western Railway, it also served as a terminus for the North Devon & Cornwall Junction Light Railway to Halwill. The station is still here, although today it is fully licensed and open as a pub. Reminders of the railway have returned, too. The creation of a railway preservation society has seen a short section of track re-laid near the platforms, allowing rolling stock to be displayed.

Heading south through delightful woodland we emerge 2 miles along at Watergate Halt. The name has no connection to the US scandal of the 1970s; it is simply a small station where the platform was little more than the length of a carriage. There was, however, a small siding used to transport livestock, materials and machinery to the local farm.

Shortly before the next station we reach the high point at Peters Marland. A wooden sculpture marks the exact spot and further examples of this artwork can be found in the benches. It has been just over 2 miles from Watergate to East Yarde, past Yarde Orchard which abounds in woodland plants, particularly during the spring.

Yarde Halt was constructed as an intermediate halt in 1925. Initially, it served the clay works but soon became a request stop for passengers. Today, the Yarde Cafe occupies the site, along with space for half a dozen cars. Caterers are proud to tell customers over and over again that their produce is sourced locally, and very good it is too, although the cafe is only open during the warmer months.

Petrockstowe is 4 miles from East Yarde. Along the way the carved wooden benches give way to mosaic seats which all display a wildlife theme. There is an old station along here at Marland Works; however, it is difficult to find evidence of it now. It was built as part of the Torrington & Marland Railway, a narrow

Torrington Station in 1960 when trains were being worked mainly by LMS-type Ivatt 2MT 2-6-2Ts, one of which is seen approaching on a train from Barnstaple Junction. (*Courtesy of Dr Ben Brooksbank*)

gauge line built to carry bricks and clay. In 1925 it became part of the main line and today it is a favourite target for industrial railway historians.

When arriving at Petrockstowe the sharp-eyed may notice that the name of the railway station was always spelled Petrockstow, without the final 'e'. The reason is simple: when the line was narrow gauge and carried ball clay, the original timetable was produced by Colonel Stevens, who made the name appear with only eleven letters. Thus, a misprint on the timetable changed the spelling of the station's name. Note that the station remains a mile outside the village of Petrockstowe and there were once two platforms.

By the time we reach Meeth we have travelled a total of 46 miles. There is no doubt of the station here for the name of Meeth Halt and the platform with its concrete shelter are quite evident. As this is the terminus for the Tarka Trail and a section of the National Cycle Network, there are plans to renovate the station to a standard befitting its status. Indeed, it will probably attain a prominence post-Beeching which it could never have hoped to achieve before the rails were removed.

21   WHITBY TO SCARBOROUGH

Twenty-one miles of the most scenic pathways in the land parallel the coastline of Yorkshire. Commonly known as the Cinder Track, as the ballast was made from cinders and not the usual crushed stone, almost every mile of this old railway offers something new for the traveller.

The line was originally planned to be a continuation of the North Yorkshire Moors Railway, but this proved a little ambitious for the available funding and thus it has become a popular route for walkers. Nevertheless, plans to reopen it as a rail link along the coast have not been abandoned entirely. It is hoped that heritage railway and footpath could run side by side, a certain boost for the local economy.

The line was opened on 16 July 1885, carrying both passengers and freight until its closure in 1965. Unusually, British Rail organised the lifting of the line themselves, funds from scrap filling their coffers. Just why BR decided to dismantle this line when so many others were contracted out is unclear, although there are stories of the line being poorly maintained, suggesting BR were hoping to hide their shortcomings.

The last scheduled train ran on 6 March 1965. The diesel-hauled train comprising seven coaches departed Scarborough at 14.47. Between 300 and 400 passengers were on board, including 100 members of the Scarborough Round Table. A special full of train enthusiasts had left Manchester that morning and arrived at Whitby mid-afternoon. Half an hour after arrival the special returned to York via the Esk Valley, Goathland and Pickering.

Almost immediately after these last trains had departed the line, it was noticed that several items had been removed as mementoes by persons unknown. The list included the station nameplate from Flying Hall Station. Others took the trouble to ask for something to remember the line by. Driver Albert Clarkson was thanked personally by a local woman, whose home backed on to the line; she had received answering whistles to her waves for more years than she cared to remember.

We shall follow the trail from Whitby, where it starts near the Community College. For the first mile the trail is fairly uneventful; quite flat as it runs south until it suddenly begins to climb. In the next mile it climbs to twice its starting height reaching 330ft above sea level. Shortly before the 2-mile mark it hits the Larpool Viaduct, a massive construction which was clearly never intended to take walkers, horse riders and cyclists over the River Esk. There are thirteen brick-built spans which soar to a maximum of 120ft above the tidal river, with a span of 915ft. Designed by John Waddell, this Grade II listed construction crosses the present Esk Valley line upon reaching the southern shore.

From here the line swings south-east and continues up a slight gradient until it reaches Hawsker Station at approximately 440ft above sea level. Hawsker Station closed on 8 March 1965, but is open today and probably doing as much business as it has ever done. However, there are no day returns sold here in the twenty-first century; today it is home to Trailways Cycle Hire where you can hire every conceivable bicycle. Irrespective of age and ability there is something to suit everyone: tandems are available, as are baby buggies which attach to the back of an adult bike and are fully enclosed to protect junior from the inclement weather. A recently refurbished carriage offers self-catering accommodation, with views over Robin Hood's Bay. These beaches are just half a mile away. A second carriage contains a museum of both the former railway and its present-day use as a leisure path.

The Larpool Viaduct. (*Author*)

It is another 3 miles to the next station on the old line: Robin Hood's Bay. The route takes us closer to the sea and, as we would expect, heads downhill once more. It drops to 180ft on a gradient of 1 in 43 and leads almost to the edge of the cliffs, which afford spectacular views over the bay and the delightfully named Boggle Hole and Stoupe Beck Sands further along the coast. A slight incline brings us to the station itself.

The station served the fishing port of Robin Hood's Bay as much for freight as for passenger traffic. The old photographs show a 1½-ton crane in the yard capable of lifting substantial loads. The yard, the largest on the line, included a weighbridge, coal yard, cattle dock, goods shed, sidings, and a signal box – which is why freight services were withdrawn from here three months after the rest of the line. The main station on the up line still survives, although only the near end of the down platform can be seen today. The station building and stationmaster's house now provide holiday accommodation, yet there were four camping coaches in a siding here before the closure of the station in 1965.

Continuing south, a series of gentle undulations brings us to the start of a climb which will eventually lead to the highest part of the track. However, first we come to Flying Hall Station, a little over 2 miles from Robin Hood's Bay and moving away from the coast once more. Little is left of Flying Hall Station; it is possible to make out a little of both platforms and the station house is now a private residence.

The line swings back east and then follows the coast south-east. This is a long climb to the highest point of the line just beyond Ravenscar Station at 631ft. The views from here are unsurpassed, including that over Peak Alum, which is why the station was originally called Peak on the plans but renamed by the time it opened on 1 October 1897.

Peak Alum claims to be the birthplace of the chemical industry, at least in Britain. Local rock was combined with human urine to make alum, used to fix dye in cloth making. While this process had been known for years, Peak Alum was the first to produce alum commercially in volume. While the rock could be quarried here in vast amounts, the other ingredient was a problem, for the population was very small. This was solved by the North Sea, which allowed barges to be brought up from London carrying huge quantities of urine from the capital. The process is chronicled at the Peak Alum Works, now an informative museum.

Ravenscar was home to a fourth-century signalling beacon, one of a chain erected along the east coast by the Romans. The original track does not cross this but heads underground through a tunnel. Ravenscar is actually better known for what was never there. The train service brought visitors to a coastline which had previously only been seen by fishermen; tourists were restricted to either Scarborough or Whitby. The railway was seen as the catalyst for expansion and plans were laid out to develop a brand-new resort here. Roads were cut, sewers

The spectacular view across Robin Hood's Bay. (*Author*)

installed and homes were built. But the distance from here to the beach deterred visitors and the venture failed. The houses and the streets, although somewhat overgrown, are still visible, and the railway has left its mark on the map in the form of the only surviving street name – Station Square.

Ravenscar Station marks the point just past halfway; from here the line drops 300ft over the next 4 miles, running almost parallel to the coast until we arrive at Hayburn Wyke. Originally opened in 1887, the platform was on the up side of the track. The North East Region Railways complained that the platform had been constructed from wood and so a second platform was built on the down side.

The stationmaster's house at Hayburn Wyke was not built until 1892; prior to this he stayed in a local hotel. In 1953 the station ceased to be staffed and was reduced to a halt. Finally closing in 1965, little remains of the station aside from some fencing and concrete supports. The stationmaster's house is now a private dwelling and a small brick building alongside is thought to be the old booking office.

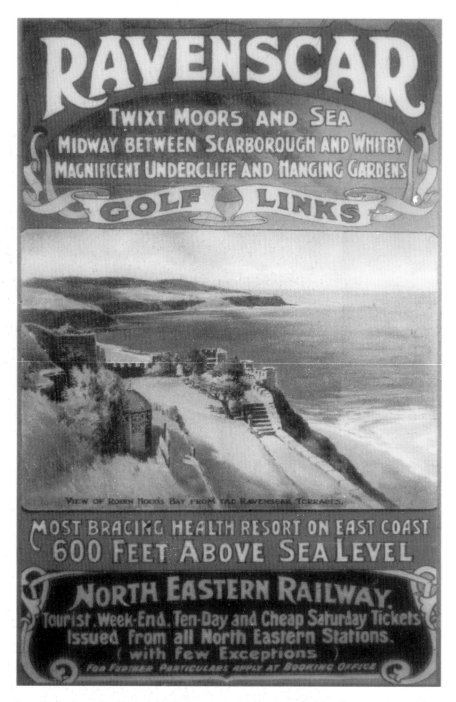

A reminder from the days when Ravenscar was planned as a holiday destination – a proposition which never materialised. (*Author*)

1 Former GWR 060 pannier tank engine No. 1369 emerges from its cloud of steam as it runs around to run backwards from Buckfastleigh to Totnes. (*Author*)

2 The extensive station yard at Buckfastleigh from the footbridge. (*Author*)

3 Cloughton Station is now, as the sign indicates, a tea room, a B&B and self-catering accommodation. (*Author*)

4 Former stationmaster Alfred Hart would be as proud of the immaculate gardens at Cloughton Station today as he was in the days when he was a prize winner. (*Author*)

5 A modern marker on the Cinder Track at Ravenscar. (*Author*)

6 The ornate platform edge at Ravenscar. (*Author*)

7 The unmistakeable image of a rural railway station can still be seen at Hawsker, where self-catering accommodation and cycle hire are available. (*Author*)

8 A sign indicates the Cinder Track, which runs along the old Whitby to Scarborough railway line. (*Author*)

9 One of three daily services passes beneath the Larpool Viaduct having departed Whitby. (*Author*)

10 The signal box and level crossing at Levisham. (*Author*)

11 *Cock o' the North* pulls the train out of Grosmont Station. (*Author*)

12 The picturesque Rothley Station on a sunny day in 2012. (*Author*)

13 A delightful gas-style electric light at Carrog Station. (*Author*)

14 A copy of a poster challenging the Beeching Axe falling on Goathland. (*Author*)

15 A Santa Special pulls into Swanwick Junction. (*Courtesy of the Midland Railway Trust Ltd*)

16 The longest and southernmost tunnel on the Monsal Trail. (*Author*)

17 Breathtaking views from Headstone Viaduct. (*Author*)

Two miles further on, skirting Cloughton Woods, we come to the former Cloughton Station. Of all the stations on this line these buildings are in the best condition and are still in daily use: the station building now offers bed and breakfast accommodation, while the stationmaster's house is a delightful tearoom. There is also Oscar, a luxury railway carriage, refurbished to offer self-catering accommodation – this could also be considered a victim of the Beeching cuts as it was built at Derby in 1962. Some of the platforms remain, as does a renovated goods shed and a signal, which is the most obvious indication that a railway once ran through here.

Before departing, take a look around the small garden. Fifty years ago this was the pride and joy of stationmaster Alfred Hart. The last train out of Cloughton marked the end of Alfred's career with the railways, for he was retiring at the end of March after forty-five years in the job, of which the last nineteen were at Cloughton.

Leaving school at 13 he followed his father into the family business making shoes. It was not long before Alfred realised this was not the career for him and he took a job as a signal boy at Flamborough in 1920. He moved to similar jobs at Wharram and Sherburn-in-Elmet, before coming to Scarborough as a ticket collector. Spells at Leeds and Burton Agnes ensued before he was placed at York as relief stationmaster.

During his time at York Alfred was a member of the railway gymnasium and represented the goods team at cricket. In 1941 he moved to Barton Hill where he was put in charge of ammunition movements – responsible for train loads of some 200 tons every day – until the end of the war. He was also secretary of the War Savings Committee and helped raise over the £2,000 target. This resulted in recognition from Buckingham Palace after the war and he was invited to a march past and garden party.

During his two decades at Cloughton, Alfred Hart won twenty of his twenty-eight first prizes in station garden competitions. Modestly, he shared the praise with other workers, who also took great pride in the appearance of their station, even continuing to do so in the final year despite the station being listed for closure.

Another 3 miles further south and we come to Scalby. This station was closed to regular traffic on 2 March 1953, although occasional trains stopped here until the line finally closed in 1964. Scalby Station no longer exists and the development of Chichester Close occupies the same site east of the viaduct. Scalby Viaduct carried the line across the Scalby Beck – a much smaller construction than Larpool Viaduct outside Whitby but still a substantial four arches.

After passing the former Gallows Close goods yard, now the car park for Sainsbury's, the line once headed into Falsgrave Tunnel. Today this is bricked up for safety reasons and it is no longer possible to follow the route with any great accuracy to end at the former Scarborough Londesborough Road Station.

Following the closure of the line debates continued to rumble on. Dissenters pointed out the inadequate public transport for residents and suggested buses would be incapable of navigating some of the climbs and turns on the road during the worst of the weather. Furthermore, during the first part of the 1960s, the sixteen weeks of the summer season had seen no fewer than 150,000 passengers arriving by rail to Whitby alone. No bus service could ever cope with such numbers, and this did not take into account visitors to Robin Hood's Bay, Scarborough, and other points along the coast.

Even the train service had problems with the landscape at times. One example of this occurred during the bad weather of February 1947. The first train from Scarborough on the 11th got stuck in a snowdrift near Staintondale; it was eventually rescued and returned to its starting point. For more than a week

The arrow-straight path is a tell-tale indication of a former railway line. (*Author*)

no trains travelled this line until, within hours of it reopening, a goods train heading for Whitby became trapped in a drift between Scalby and Cloughton. A rescue engine hauled away the rolling stock and freed the locomotive by thawing out the iced-up moving parts with no little assistance from the steam from the boiler.

22 CUCKOO LINE

The name of the Cuckoo Line has been passed to the trail now that the track has been lifted. An odd name for a railway line, the reason is said to be because Heathfield was heralded as the first place in the country to hear the returning cuckoo in spring each year. This was not just folklore, for as close as possible to 14 April each year, at the Heffle Cuckoo Fair in Heathfield, a lady would release a cuckoo from her basket, symbolising the first 'cuckoo of spring'.

The line itself began as the London, Brighton & South Coast Railway. It was created in two sections: one from Polegate to Hailsham, opened on 14 May 1849; the other, to Eridge, saw the first traffic in September 1880, effectively creating a direct line between Eastbourne and London.

Our 14-mile journey through the East Sussex countryside begins at Polegate, although not at its current station of four platforms. Neither will we start at the original station, for this no longer exists, swept away by the present stop which is the third creation at Polegate. Our target is the second station, still to be found a quarter of a mile south of here, which was constructed in 1881. A pub and restaurant occupies the substantial former station building, its size an indication of the importance of this junction. It is not difficult to find as it is known as Old Polegate Station. Parts of one of the platforms can still be made out.

Having travelled 3 miles from Polegate we come to the former Hailsham Station. In 1860 approval was given to link Hailsham through Uckfield with Haywards Heath via the Ouse Valley Railway. Despite construction being started, and still quite evident in the form of embankments and bridges, the work was never completed. Opened in 1849, the last train left this station at 22.30 on 8 September 1968. All that remains of the former station is a concrete wall west of the site supporting the embankment, while the site of the station itself is now occupied by a housing estate.

The line to Hailsham closed three years after the rest of the line and was hotly disputed by all concerned. Even British Rail saw Hailsham as a growing community and trains as the only logical way to commute. Car travel was not as commonplace as today, and any bus service would prove inadequate considering the ever-increasing numbers involved.

Passing through Hailsham we cross Upper Horsbridge Road. This section of the line closed in April 1968 when a lorry damaged the bridge and, with the line earmarked for closure just eleven days after the accident, it never reopened. However, it is possible to continue on the 1½ miles to the next stop – Hellingly – be it on foot or bicycle.

Hellingly Station still exists, complete with the distinctive canopy, stained-glass windows and ornate plasterwork. It is now a private residence beyond the undeveloped area once occupied by sidings. Opposite this, a light railway once operated between the station and Hellingly Psychiatric Hospital. Constructed in 1899 it utilised a saddle tank locomotive to transport materials to build the line, which itself was to bring both passengers and coal to the hospital. The line was electrified within three years, two fully laden wagons and a single twelve-seater tramcar being pulled by a locomotive rumoured to be imported from Germany. While coal was brought for the hospital's boilers until 1959, the boilers were adapted for the much cleaner oil; the passenger tramcar had been abandoned in 1931 as uneconomical. The platform serving that link was removed two years later.

It is a distance of 4½ miles to Horum. Here, it is the station platform and not the track that forms the bed of the route, while the concrete sign is still in place. On the way, keep your eyes open for fauna and particularly flora – purple orchids grow alongside the trackbed in the spring and a familiar aroma may be detected if the wind is light and blowing in the right direction. This will be ramson, or wild garlic, the name derived from the Old English *hramsa*. Note that the hamlet grew up around the station; there was little here before the coming of the railway.

Two miles further on and we come to Heathfield. The station, built in 1880, still survives as part of an industrial estate, a large car park, and a shop which occupies the former booking office. Shortly afterwards we come to Harefield Tunnel; almost 300yd in length, it is lit to enable walkers and cyclists to pass through safely. When the original station was built it was a mile away from the settlement, which quickly relocated from what is now known as Old Heathfield.

Emerging we arrive at Mayfield Station, presently a private residence but still in a rather rundown condition. Very little remains of the station embankment and platforms: it was cleared in the 1970s to make way for the bypass and what is left is completely overgrown. The goods yard has been entirely redeveloped and a new housing estate exists.

Ahead is another hill which is negotiated by way of the Mayfield Tunnel. This is not what it seems, for the 'tunnel' is effectively a long bridge. Stretched out beneath the A267 at an acute angle, it is, in reality, only 50yd long.

Of all the benefits emerging from the Beeching Axe, this tunnel came to feature in an iconic British television show. On 5 September 1967, just two years after the last train passed through, the cult television series *The Prisoner* made its bow on our screens. Surprisingly, only seventeen episodes of the series were ever made, but on 4 February 1968 the lead character, Number Six, played by Patrick McGoohan, made an escape by driving through a long tunnel, smashing through the wooden gates at the end and emerging into bright sunlight. As many will know, the series was filmed at the Welsh resort of Portmeirion, yet the tunnel was none other than the one found at Mayfield. As breaking free marked the end of *The Prisoner*, this has become a place of pilgrimage for those who gave the series cult status, something nobody could ever have foreseen.

Rotherfield was the next stop on the line. The station, officially known as Rothfield & Mark Cross, is still standing and now a private residence in Station Close, off Station Road. As with Mayfield, the last train ran in June 1965 and the goods yard has been redeveloped.

Approaching Eridge, the sound of metal train wheels crossing points may be heard. This is not the sound of a ghostly train, but a reminder that Eridge Station is still open and links with the Wealden line and the Oxted line. Indeed, rather than facing closure this important commuter junction is seeing its single platform increased to three.

The heritage lines and sustainable transport networks have kept many arteries open and prevented them from becoming overgrown; however, this route has recently become the subject of an ambitious and exciting project. For the first time in the fifty years since Beeching, a significant stretch of the branch line is being seen as the answer to the age-old problem of overcrowded roads. While there will certainly be an attempt to attract heritage railway enthusiasts, the principal idea is to reintroduce a line which is both profitable and sustainable. How long will it be before walkers and cyclists see the reintroduction of a regular train service between Heathfield and East Grinstead?

When it comes to sustainability the organisers should be congratulated for using storm-damaged trees only for the many benches and resting points along the route, principally used by walkers. The cuckoo theme is also seen in the fauna growing alongside the trail. Lady's Smock, also known as the Cuckoo Flower, is identifiable by the pale mauve flower of four petals appearing in the damper places in spring. The plant is a favourite of the Orange Tip butterfly, another visitor to the trail. Similarly, Lords and Ladies has the alternative name of Cuckoo Pint: the glossy, arrow-shaped leaves are overshadowed by a white flower which eventually turns black, before green berries ripen to a reddish-orange in the autumn. Do not be tempted to eat these, they are poisonous. The dunnock, a sparrow-like bird, is found in some numbers, and its nest in the hedgerows does play host to the eggs of the cuckoo.

Today, the route sees some 200,000 users per annum; note this is a rough estimation as it is impossible to count everyone. People join and leave the trail at many different places and numbers could well be significantly higher. It is used as a traffic-free route by many schoolchildren to their place of education. Along the route they may pass one of the six wooden sculptures depicting the trail's wildlife and history. These also act as mileposts.

Rerouting to the north has meant it has been impossible to link this path with the Forest Way at Groombridge. However, Sustrans continues to work to convince the county council it would be possible to link the two former railway routes using an on-road route in the short term.

23   SOMERSET & DORSET JOINT RAILWAY

Railways of today appear purpose-built, yet this is misleading. They invariably began as smaller segments which were joined together, just as the smaller railway companies did to form increasingly larger networks. Similarly, when in operation the Somerset & Dorset Joint Railway (S&DJR) was as different from other lines then as it is today, for it was very much a bits-and-pieces railway, linking together pieces of other lines to bring passengers to the south coast. For this reason it was much loved by railway enthusiasts for its constantly changing scenery. Today, those who hope to save something of the line continue to work independently of each other, only loosely coordinated under the banner of the S&DJR.

The Beeching Axe fell on this line in 1966. Ironically, the line had never been more successful than in the first half of the 1960s, but it was apparently not successful enough to avert closure. Undoubtedly it was the inconsistency of passenger numbers that highlighted the line, which, despite its name, brought trains from as far north as Manchester – although these Manchester trains were limited to a few local daily services and a single daily long-distance service. Passenger numbers may have looked good but a much larger-than-normal percentage travelled long distance on summer Saturdays when trains were packed almost to overflowing. A very different story was seen on any other day.

As already stated, this line is the unification of shorter lengths. Of course, this is true of most main lines but only the S&DJR still looks as if it was created in this way and retains the sharp edges which would normally have been smoothed out. Among the lines which combined to form the S&DJR is the Somerset Railway. Opened in 1854 it connected Glastonbury with Highbridge Wharf and was built to carry goods from Glastonbury to the Bristol Channel port at a distance of some 18 miles. An extension to Burnham, hoping to attract passengers as well as freight, saw a 900ft-long slipway topped with piers jutting out into the tidal waters. The idea was simple: whatever the level of the tide, the boat would meet the train at the optimum height for loading and unloading. In practice the arrangement was awkward and soon abandoned. A second extension the following year, 1859, saw Wells connected to the network.

At this time the line was still operating on a broad gauge track and continued to do so for a number of years. It was when the link to Cole was first laid that the odd sight of mixed gauges was seen. Three rails enabled broad gauge traffic to negotiate the same route as the standard gauge, although this did not last for long. Cole was not an important junction; that it provided a meeting place between the Somerset line and the Dorset Central Railway was, at the time, its only importance.

The Dorset Railway opened in November 1860 between Wimborne and Blandford. The London & South Western Railway operated here and it was hoped to link the line to Bath and thus the north. This was eventually realised through amalgamation with the Somerset Railway, which came into being by an Act of Parliament in 1862. By the early nineteenth century, the line's long-term goal of Bournemouth was reached. This was to prove the real winner in later years, bringing countless holidaymakers to this popular resort on the south coast.

It was vital to connect this line to a direct link to London. This was achieved by a junction at Templecombe on the Salisbury and Yeovil line. The problem of

Highbridge, and the train to Evercreech prepares to depart in 1962. (*Courtesy of Dr Ben Brooksbank*)

the two lines being on different levels was solved by taking the trains to the east. Clearly not the ideal answer, although it does show there was no intention to run trains straight through in these early days.

Eventually the issue was resolved by having the S&DJR running through Templecombe Lower Station, with the Upper Station handling London traffic. A shuttle service was operated between the two by the Salisbury & Yeovil Railway to prevent passengers having to walk half a mile. This temporary solution was improved upon in several stages until the early part of the nineteenth century.

At the end of August 1863, the dream of linking the Bristol Channel with the English Channel while avoiding the dangerous coastline of Devon and Cornwall was realised. This was not the final piece to the puzzle, the most notable addition being the extension to Bath. Passenger numbers were supported by freight traffic, particularly from the Somerset coalfields, which continued until closure following the Beeching Report.

Some of the sections have reopened as heritage lines. Two – the East Somerset Railway and the West Somerset Railway – are dealt with under their chapters. Nearly half a century later other lengths are being developed by Dorset Countryside as pathways and cycle routes. While the route could well be extended, currently there are just five sections wholly within Dorset, totalling a little over 7 miles, each with its own character and offering something different.

Running from west to east the route begins at Stalbridge. So far less than half a mile has been developed but is used regularly as an environmentally friendly route to work and/or school. The site of the station itself is now home to an industrial estate. What was a single line with a passing loop, goods shed and signal box has disappeared, although the sharp-eyed may spot the rails still embedded in the road. The next section begins at Sturminster Newton and runs for 4 miles. What was a station of two platforms with shelters, a passing loop, small goods yard and signal box, is now a trading estate and an area of parkland. However, there are metal gates at the entrance to this area which remind us this was once the property of the S&DJR.

Near here the route allows access to Fiddleford Manor, a stone-built manor house built around 1370 for the then Sheriff of Somerset and Dorset, William Latimer. With several additions over the ensuing centuries, particularly the sixteenth and eighteenth centuries, the property is now owned by English Heritage and open to the public.

Approximately halfway along we reach Shillingstone, the last surviving station of the former Dorset Central Railway. With the ancient hill fort at Hambledon Hill above and the Stour flowing below, this is certainly a picturesque location. But this is not the only reason why it is the most ornate station on the line. Much of the decor must have been to impress a very important traveller.

During its operational history Shillingstone frequently saw the Prince of Wales, the future Edward VII, as a passenger on his way to parties at Iwerne Minster

House. The poet Rupert Brooke, who had been stationed at Blandford Camp, also passed through the station. His unit marched here to board the train for Avonmouth before joining the troopship bound for Gallipoli. He never returned.

In a uniquely British way the station had its own greenhouse. Here, staff, and in particular the stationmaster, nurtured seedlings and young plants until they were ready for the garden. Alighting from the trains, visitors were immediately confronted with a splendid display, the high standard of which never wavered.

The Shillingstone Railway Project continues to work to restore this section. Their ultimate goal is to operate trains here once more. While nobody can forecast exactly when that will be, their website at www.shillingstone.addr.com includes a clock which counts every day, hour, minute and second since the last train departed the station.

Another short section of only half a mile is open through Blandford. This short section allows pedestrian access between here and Blandford St Mary. Nothing remains of Blandford Station; the site has been developed as a housing estate. Enthusiasts are recreating the site at Blandford Museum where a 1/76th working scale model is nearing completion at the time of writing.

There follows a short break and then the final section of 2½ miles to Spetisbury via Charlton Marshall and its halts. The latter station is still quite evident. Both short platforms are visible in the shadow of the road bridge, although the wooden shelters are long gone. This leg also provides access to the watercress beds for which central southern England is rightly famous.

When trains arrived at Spetisbury they would find two platforms with shelters, a station building and a signal box. Note Spetisbury Station, opened in 1860, was relegated to the status of a halt in 1934. The station features in plans to restore the Somerset & Dorset Railway as a twenty-first-century transport service. Backers have made it clear there will also be a heritage element, including the running of steam specials – a virtual guarantee of passenger numbers.

Historically, this was a line of bits and pieces and today those pieces have never been more fragmented. Yet the enthusiasm for the line in its many guises remains unabated and the success of whatever is undertaken in the future seems assured.

24   MAWDDACH TRAIL

As discussed in the chapter on the Llangollen Railway, there is a 10-mile stretch between Dolgellau and Barmouth which is now a bridleway and cycle route known as the Mawddach Trail, or *Llwybr Mawddach* in Welsh. Together with the narrow gauge railway at Bala, the three connected routes show different aspects of former lines in the principality.

This is one of the most popular routes for both walkers and cyclists. And it is no wonder considering the splendour of the valley of the Afon Mawddach, where the river meanders over a comparatively short route, opening out at the estuary where a bridge leads across to Barmouth. A word of caution for those intending to follow this route: this is the Mawddach Trail and not the Mawddach Way. The former is almost perfectly level and a little short of 10 miles; it can be walked both ways in a day and is even designated as wheelchair accessible. The latter is a circular path around the estuary, is unsuitable for cycles, covers over 30 miles and climbs to a high point of over 1,100ft above sea level; experts advise you allow three days to cover this challenging route.

Back to our chosen route and we shall begin at Dolgellau in the Snowdonia National Park. From the former location of the station, known by its Welsh name only since 12 September 1960 (previously the Anglicised version of Dolgelly), we shall follow the southern bank of the Afon Mawddach to the estuary. This is an ever-changing and peaceful journey, the river cutting between the Rhinog Hills on one side and the Cadair Idris massif on the other.

The town of Dolgellau has plenty to offer with over 200 listed buildings in its narrow streets. Dolgellau Station was opened on 4 August 1868, at a point where two former railway empires met head on: the huge Great Western Railway and the smaller Cambrian Railway Company, which built the route we shall follow. By the time it closed there were two platforms with a passing loop and an extensive goods yard with a turntable. There is no sign of the station today; it disappeared when the A494 Dolgellau bypass was constructed in the 1970s. The line was intended to bring the tourists into Barmouth from as far afield as Birmingham and Manchester, along a line which connected the West Midlands with the Welsh coast in the shadow of Snowdonia National Park. However, local businesses soon took advantage of the artery to ship their own goods into the rich markets of England. Dolgellau's weavers soon benefited from the larger market, and slate also made use of the line, as we shall see further along the route.

The first river is not the Mawddach – we shall come to that shortly. Here the river is the Wnion (almost pronounced 'onion'), a brisk and pleasant stream which tumbles over the rocks and stones on its way to join its larger cousin. It is only half a mile along the footpath to the next landmark, the Wernddu footbridge, taking us across the river to the trail proper, for it was along the north bank that the trains ran. Shortly afterwards we pass a reed bed, a site of special scientific interest which claims to be the largest reed bed in the principality.

Look across to the northern shore and you will see the Welsh Yukon: the gold-mining industry was born here in the 1860s, and has been reborn time and again until as recently as 1998. Doubtless another vein will be discovered before long and, for a short period at least, gold mining will come back to the valley. The quality of the metal is among the finest in the world – no royal wedding in memory has not used some Welsh gold in the rings worn by bride and groom.

Another half a mile and we arrive at the next station, which was Penmaen-pool. As with the previous station it had two platforms and a passing loop, but unlike Dolgellau part of the station is still here; indeed, some buildings are still in use. The old platforms are now a car park. Those parked here may not be walking the trail; they could be here to see the station's old signal box, still painted in the GWR colours of cream and brown, and now used as an information centre and observation post for the Royal Society for the Protection of Birds. Alongside the signal box is the Penmaenpool Wooden Toll Bridge, built in 1879. It replaced the earlier ferry and was largely funded by money from the gold mines.

The toll bridge is a Cadw-registered building – Cadw being the official body for the preservation of historic sites in Wales. The old stationmaster's house, ticket office and waiting room are still here and have been converted into an annexe for the George III Hotel. Here we see a perfectly preserved signal with a warning sign to those who might trespass on the track, stating: 'DANGER. Survivors will be prosecuted.'

Leaving the station there is an incline leading past the buildings which served the station and sidings. The trackbed runs through a cutting blasted out of the rock to provide a gradient suitable for a railway. Travelling on we head directly west to meet with the river estuary. It is this stretch which is of particular interest to birdwatchers, who can view waders in the mudflats on one side and an excellent variety of woodland birds on the other.

As the River Mawddach dominates the route we should say a few words about a river which is probably little known outside Snowdonia. In 1976 the flooding river washed away much of the surviving ballast from the trackbed, effectively producing the present pathway at a stroke. Six significant tributaries – Afon Cwm Mynach, Afon Gamlan, Afon Eden, Afon Gain, Afon Wen, and the aforementioned Afon Wnion – and many smaller streams drain a sizable area. Each river has its own character, from providing important habitats for mosses and liverwort to gold mining and panning.

It may seem hard to believe when walking through this idyllic scenery in the twenty-first century, but the river has suffered greatly from pollution in the past. From artillery ranges, munitions storage and the preparation of animal skins to its function as a major shipbuilding centre in the eighteenth century, all contributed to the pollution. Yet today it is an important fishery for trout and salmon, despite the relatively high acidity levels washed in from the peat soils on the hills. The number and size of the tributaries mean the river is liable to flood during and after the heaviest downpours. Indeed, as already stated, the track ballast was washed away by one flood, assisting the development of the track for walkers and cyclists.

Crossing one bridge across a tributary we come to a straight section of track where the embankment has been built to cut through the estuary itself. Waters have access points all along to accommodate the rise and ebb of the tides. Still we see the old telegraph poles which stand alongside the railway lines the length and breadth of the land.

Returning to dry land once more, this southern shore is, and always has been, largely agricultural. Farm buildings built of local stone blend in perfectly with the walls bordering the small fields where sheep graze. Concrete tank traps remain, still defending the estuary from potential invasion seven decades after they were erected. These are no eyesore, perhaps owing to the trees which now camouflage the regular shapes, and there is a distinct impression of a row of teeth, ready to bite at the enemy should he try to invade via the estuary.

It is a little more than 3 miles from the previous station to Arthog. There are many picnic stops on the way and the easy walking and delightful views mean this is hardly the most strenuous exercise. Arthog, like Dolgellau, has no surviving station buildings, although the location of the platforms can still be made out.

Arthog was a mining community, not for gold but slate. The rows of workers' cottages are a pretty picture, something which cannot be said of the scar left by the workings of the slate quarries, although these are invisible except from the air. Arthog Station, with its picnic area and car park, is opposite a pathway marking the line where trams brought slate from the mine to the railway and thereafter to Barmouth and beyond.

The railway then leaves the shoreline and runs straight for a good mile through an avenue of trees, which is highly reminiscent of a railway line. We loop around to the right and ahead of us is the station which was Barmouth Junction.

There are two tramways which are worthy of mention, visible to those who keep their eyes open for a fairly obvious embankment. Solomon Andrews tried to found a holiday resort here in the 1890s. His plans were grand but he achieved little; the few houses he did build are now private homes and set away from the main walk. One tramway brought building materials in to this part of the estuary; the second is found just short of the bridge at the mouth and is quite evident on the right.

For some time the bridge across the mouth of the estuary to Barmouth has been glimpsed, but first we must pass through the junction station of Morfa Mawddach. The old station platforms sit alongside a still active line between Pwllheli and Machynlleth. This line crosses the bridge alongside the footpath. It is a toll bridge and its revenue helped to reopen it to all but the heaviest rail traffic after the teredo marine worm burrowed into the wooden piles and almost brought it down. It is three-quarters of a mile in length, the longest bridge in Wales, and one of the most instantly recognisable features in the entire principality.

The bridge has a wooden section of 113 spans and an iron section of just eight spans. This latter part once slid aside to allow the passage of ships in and out of the estuary. This was not popular with the railway, for it took thirty-seven minutes to open and close, added to which was the time it took to get the ship through the opening. The modern version is a swing bridge, one which has not moved for

A rare image of Morfa Mawddach. (*Courtesy of Dr Ben Brooksbank*)

over twenty years. Each of these columns was sunk 120ft below sea level through the silt and mud to stand on the bedrock below.

Barmouth, or *Abermaw* in Welsh, appears to be clinging precariously on to the edge of the land between the hills and the water. As stated at the beginning, this is linked to another chapter – that of the Llangollen Railway. The link is completed at Barmouth in the form of the station's old signal box, which became redundant following the introduction of radio signalling. It was removed and erected at Glyndyfrdwy Station on the heritage Llangollen Railway.

25   CASTLEMAN TRAILWAY

The Castleman Trailway is known as 'trailway' because while all of its length is passable by foot, there is a short section which is not available to cyclists. This circuitous route is named after nineteenth-century solicitor Charles Castleman, who suggested the line would do better serving as many places as possible at a time when its eventual destination, Bournemouth, was little more than a small village.

A trail of some 16 miles, it roughly follows something of the former Southampton & Dorchester Railway, specifically the line between Brockenhurst, Ringwood and Hamworthy Junction. The railway opened in 1847, when it was known as the Castleman Corkscrew, and is still open today as far as Lymington Junction. The route from there to Hamworthy Junction was closed in May 1964 to passengers, and to freight the following year when the track was lifted. The trailway, formed from the old railway line and a number of roads, forms an oval. While such a shape has no true starting point, there are two centres: at Bickerley Road in Ringwood and the car park at Upton Country Park.

From Bickerley Road the trailway heads west, skirting Watchmoor Wood to the north before turning south-west. Soon the route, now heading arrow straight, comes through a corner of Ashley Heath, past Lions Hill and into woodland once more before reaching West Moors. Having passed through West Moors, the track diverts – as shown by its unique waymarkers – north along the road and alongside the West Moors Woodland & Nature Reserve. It then unites with the Ferndown, Stour and Forest Trail and back to the line of the former railway at Ameysford.

The trail does not follow the route of the dismantled railway but heads through Uddens Wood to Stapehill. The way heads for Little Canford and then along the scenic route of the banks of the River Stour. After this, the route leaves the railway and the river to follow the A341 road south through Oakley to Dunyeats Hill and Broadstone, where it rejoins the line of the dismantled railway once more. Finally, as we leave Broadstone and the former trackbed, the road heads south to cross the A35 and reach Upton Country Park.

This is one of the gentlest of the former railway routes, with hardly an incline to trouble either walker or cyclist.

26 REALISING THE DREAM

Beeching or not, the days of steam were numbered. However, his report did nurture an amazing nostalgia culture on a scale probably never seen before. Thus, Beeching's legacy did create the interest which, in turn, led to the eventual launching of the Peppercorn A1 Steam Locomotive Trust in 1990. In 2008 the dream was realised when 60163 *Tornado* became the first newly built British steam locomotive for some fifty years.

The design was, as the name states, that of Arthur Peppercorn (1889–1951). The chief mechanical designer for the London & North Eastern Railway, the A1 Class Pacific was to prove his last. This 4-6-2 was some 73ft in length, weighed over 168 tons when fully laden, had a maximum boiler pressure of 250lb per square inch and a top speed of the magical 100mph.

In March 1990 a group of enthusiasts met to discuss the feasibility of building a replica A1. It was estimated the project would cost a minimum of £500,000, rising to twice that if it took ten years. Organisers hoped to be able to roll out the new locomotive in 1998, marking fifty years since the first A1 design. In 1991 the dream took an enormous step towards reality when Peppercorn's original blueprints were found at Doncaster. However, the drawings, being old and rudimentary, carried some unusual comments, such as 'best fit' or 'special care' instead of specified tolerances, and the term 'best Yorkshire iron' was not understood. It took many hours of work to redraw and tidy up the original designs – far longer than had been anticipated.

As fundraising continued a name was needed and *Tornado* was chosen to reflect the efforts of those then engaged in the Gulf War who were flying the aeroplanes of that name. The first part of the locomotive to be found was not the engine itself but the tender. At Morpeth the rotting second tender of the *Flying Scotsman* was located. On examination the frames were declared sound and suitable for the project, so it was purchased and became the first part the team laid their hands on.

Until 1997 the various parts of the developing locomotive were held in different places across the UK – the frame plates were rolled at Scunthorpe and much of the early assembly took place at the works of the Birmingham Railway

Museum at Tyseley, with manufacturers around the Midlands making significant contributions. In 1997 the Hopetown Carriage Works, Darlington, was adapted to house the construction of *Tornado* to its completion. The keys to the new building were handed over to Mrs Dorothy Mather, the widow of the designer, in an official ceremony.

Significant progress was made over the next four years, with the smoke box, wheels, pistons, rods and major components all arriving at the assembly point. The following year problems slowed progress: various standards had changed in the fifty years since the first of this model rolled off the production line, not least the height of the locomotive, originally 1in higher than the 13ft maximum now stipulated by British Rail. All these difficulties had to be resolved if the dream of running the locomotive as a main-line engine hauling lucrative specials was to be realised.

In 2006 the all-important boiler arrived and, having been tested to the exacting standards of the manufacturers, was installed. However, this process was not completed until 11 January 2008, after which the final hydraulic test took place, where many nervous individuals awaited news that the ten-year boiler certificate had been awarded. Later that year, in August, the locomotive moved under its own steam power for the first time. After a number of main-line tests, it was repainted and unveiled before the understandably thrilled and quite emotional trust members at the National Railway Museum at York.

Tornado now hauls specials along some of the classic main-line routes and it seems the locomotive will be very busy for some time to come. Enthusiasts can travel return journeys between London and Ely, Norwich and Winchester, London and Kingswear, Canterbury and Salisbury, Southend and Canterbury, Exeter and Stratford-upon-Avon, London and Shrewsbury, London and Bath, Redhill and York, Peterborough and Broxbourne, and Ashford and Norwich.

In an interview on BBC Radio 4, chairman Mark Allatt acknowledged that the project had incurred debts, which would be paid off through tours and appearances around the land. He even went so far as to say: 'The quicker we pay that back, the quicker we can start building a new engine.'

27   TYSELEY LOCOMOTIVE WORKS

Tyseley is different from the rest of the subjects in this book because there is no obvious line here – at least no heritage line, and none which has been lifted (for a footpath and/or cycle path). In southern Birmingham the Great Western Railway (GWR) depot was constructed in the district of Tyseley in 1908, a result of the opening of the North Warwickshire line as part of the main line from

Birmingham to Bristol. This new line brought traffic directly through the south of Birmingham from Stratford-upon-Avon, a more direct line than that currently used through Lapworth – a loop on the GWR line that one wit christened the Great Way Round. None could have realised it at the time, but this made it the last main-line railway built in the United Kingdom. Later routes simply upgraded existing lines.

With traffic running as soon as it was opened it became clear the nearest major depot, at Wolverhampton's Stafford Road, was much too distant and another facility was required. Bordesley was the obvious candidate but it proved impractical, being too small and with no room for expansion. Tyseley did have both the room and land for sale sufficient to build a twin turntable (one for passenger locomotives and one for freight) and two more 65ft-diameter turntables if deemed necessary.

A twin-track coaling stage, a water-softening facility serving a 98,000-gallon water tank, a large repair depot, massive lifting gear, and full engineering facilities meant this was a major industrial site. Any repair or overhaul could be undertaken; indeed, anything short of building a locomotive from scratch was quite possible. The turntables led to twenty-eight sidings of varying lengths. Some indication of the size of this 'parking area' is given by the claim that it was capable of holding thirty-six tender engines and twenty-eight tank engines. It was never going to be as important as Stafford Road, for express trains ran through to Snow Hill and Wolverhampton, but when it opened in 1908 it was allocated seventy-two engines to pull both local trains and those south to Bristol, South Wales and the West Country.

By the mid-1950s nationalisation had made Tyseley of greater importance to the railways and over 100 engines were now stationed here – a strange mix of GWR, London, Midland & Scottish (LMS) and new British Rail designs. Thereafter, it was in decline and in 1963 the freight turntable and shed were demolished, the engineering works following the year after. With BR putting an end to steam in 1968, the last three GWR pannier tank engines disappeared, the passenger roundhouse was knocked down and Tyseley's yards looked destined for auction and probable development.

Were it not for two events in 1966, Tyseley Locomotive Works may never have existed. Patrick Whitehouse purchased 7209 *Clun Castle* and negotiated a lease to hold it here, while Birmingham City Council slapped a preservation order on the turntable. This created an island in the yard which quickly became the museum and works.

The cuts, together with BR's decision to get rid of steam, resulted in a massive number of items becoming available to collectors and enthusiasts. Patrick Whitehouse founded the company 7029 Clun Castle Ltd to enable others to contribute to the preservation of that engine. Nobody could have envisaged the numbers this attracted and soon the company had sufficient funds to expand.

The locomotive *Oliver Cromwell* hauling an excursion through Dawlish and along the scenic coastal route built by Isambard Kingdom Brunel. (*Courtesy of Benjamin S. Schwarz*)

In October 1968 the LMS engine No. 5593 *Kolhapur* became the second to be stabled at Tyseley.

The company registered the Standard Gauge Steam Trust as an educational charity. Initially, their aim was to preserve steam locomotives, but this soon expanded to include rolling stock and innumerable artefacts. With further space required, a more permanent lease was negotiated, and the Tyseley Collection and the Birmingham Railway Museum were born.

Over the next three decades progress was slow but steady. Tracks had to be replaced, water columns repaired, coaling stages rebuilt and a shed with inspection pits brought in. Eventually, in 1999, the years of work brought about one of the first achievements: to run a regular (if infrequent) steam service along a main-line network. Such was the success of this venture that the trust separated into three new, quite distinct concerns, resulting in the Tyseley Locomotive Works and Vintage Trains, together with the original Tyseley Collection.

The size of the site, its ease of accessibility from the main line, and its central location make it an ideal place to offer a skilled and full-time service overhauling and maintaining locomotives. Many private operators contract work to Tyseley and one, Fragonset Railways, moved its base of operations for charter trains here, albeit only for a short while, to take advantage of this service.

Apart from a few isolated open days the site is no longer open to the public. Ironically, the success of its maintenance operations has made operating as a museum, which contributed greatly towards its funding for more than twenty years, impractical. Also, its accessibility and size make it impossible to guarantee the safety of the public, and closing the site more often to allow more visitors would be financially unwise.

The Shakespeare Express aims to recreate the travelling experience of the holiday trains from the 1950s. Popular with families, the dining car serves traditional teas or a full three-course meal. The train travels on a main line so it is allowed to reach speeds of 75mph, although some engines are limited to 60mph – more than twice the speed limit imposed on most heritage railways.

The eighteen stations from Snow Hill to Stratford-upon-Avon each have their own character. For the latter half of the journey the line follows much of the route of its predecessor, the Stratford-upon-Avon Canal. After leaving Wootton Wawen the line passes underneath the Edstone Aqueduct, the longest in England at 475ft. It spans what was once an important salt route but is now a minor road, as well as the present railway, the River Arrow, and the former Alcester Railway. Unusually, the towpath is at the level of the canal bottom. One extraordinary link between the two was the pipe once seen beneath the iron casting. From here steam engines could tap water from the canal to refill the tanks of the locomotives.

While the Stratford-upon-Avon route is the original and the excursion most associated with the Tyseley-based company, there are other destinations. Shorter journeys to Melton Mowbray, Corby, the Cotswolds, Loughborough, Leicester, Derby and Worcester are shared with long-haul trips to the likes of London, York, Salisbury, Portsmouth (combined with a cruise around the Isle of Wight), and the famous Settle to Carlisle run.

With the success of the Tyseley maintenance operation, the trust astutely considered a similar working to be a worthwhile investment at the Stratford-upon-Avon terminus. Therefore, in October 2004 the purchase of land adjoining the station and the development of the Stratford Railway Tourist Centre and Steam Locomotive Centre was arranged. Plans for a small museum are also on the cards, assuming sufficient room can be found.

At Tyseley there are fourteen diesel-electrics in the sheds, most of which are operational, and over twenty steam-powered locomotives. Among the most notable projects undertaken here was the 5043 *Earl of Mount Edgcumbe*, returned to full working order in 2008 after restoration taking thirty years. A GWR Castle Class, it was originally named *Barbury Castle* but was renamed in 1937 after just eighteen months. Withdrawn in 1963, it was sold to the Woodham Brothers scrapyard in Barry, South Wales, and found its way to Tyseley in September 1973, where it was originally intended to be a spare boiler for *Clun Castle*. In

October 2008 *Earl of Mount Edgcumbe* moved under its own steam for the first time in forty-five years.

An Avonside 0-4-0T named *Cadbury No. 1* had spent its entire working career at Bournville Works Railway. When it closed in 1976 the engine was displayed as part of the museum at Cadbury's. Given the honour of pulling the first fare-paying steam train while on long-term loan at the Gloucestershire & Warwickshire Railway, it returned to Tyseley where it was repainted and stored, as by this time the boiler certificate had expired.

Tyseley also played a prominent role in the construction of *Tornado*, the first main-line steam engine built in Britain for fifty years and mentioned in the preceding chapter.

28   BIDEFORD & INSTOW RAILWAY

This is a possibly unique heritage story from northern Devon which started in 1848 when the line opened between Barnstaple and Fremington. Seven years later the first passenger trains were extended to Bideford in what was known as the Bideford Extension Railway, although the present Bideford Station was not opened until 1872 when the line expanded as far as Torrington.

While passenger services ceased in October 1965, freight in the form of ball clay loads continued until 1982. Ball clay is used primarily in ceramics, used to make clay pipes, and gets its name from when it was cut and gathered in 35lb blocks. The corners were rounded off in transit giving them a ball-like shape. The track was lifted in 1985 and became part of the Tarka Trail, covered in Chapter 20.

The site at Bideford is now operated solely as a museum, the rebuilt signal box and an old parcels van housing the items. Until 2006 short rides were given, but vandalism brought a halt to these services. Two years later the site closed temporarily as a housing development crept ever closer. Now developers have been warded off, the line is being returned to a condition on which services can run once more.

When the line reopens visitors will find a Parcels and Miscellaneous van and British Rail standard brake van. Motive power will be found in the shape of a Hibberd 'Planet' diesel locomotive. There is also a British Railways Mark 1 coach to be found here; however, this is the property of Devon County Council and houses the Tarka Tearooms, principally for those using the Tarka Trail. The heritage group also own the signal box at Instow. Access is limited to occasional Sundays and Bank Holidays from Easter until the end of October.

Some may recall James May's audacious attempt to run OO gauge model trains between Bideford and Barnstaple in 2009 for the BBC series *James May's*

Toy Stories. Leaving Barnstaple in the mid-afternoon, the team finally accepted defeat when their last two models burnt out shortly after midnight with the goal in sight. Two years later the BBC and James May returned to try the 9.89 miles again. In a straight race between four trains, three completed the challenge: a Hornby Intercity 125; a German-designed hydrogen-powered locomotive; and James May's own model of the most famous steam locomotive still operating, the LNER Pacific 4472 *Flying Scotsman*.

29   WHAT'S IN A NAME?

There are not many places touched by the railways in the last two centuries which do not have a Railway Inn or a Station Street. Even in locations where the cuts removed all other traces of the railway, such names can still be seen. But are there any names marking the cuts of the early 1960s? There are, in fact, a number, some of which are more obvious than others.

Roads are the most obvious; for example, the line which came down from Grimsby to Peterborough and on to London passed through Alford in Lincolnshire. The Great Northern Railway station here was lost in 1970 and the new road is now known as Beechings Way. Similarly, to the south-west in the Leicestershire village of Countesthorpe is a Beechings Close, where the gardens on the west side of the development abut the former line linking Leicester with Rugby.

Further south-east we find the port of Lowestoft on the Suffolk coast. Lowestoft North Station was on the Norfolk & Suffolk Joint Railway line: this closed in 1970 and developers pointed to the culprit by naming Beeching Drive. Planners love to find a theme for their road names, even when none exists, and named Stephenson's Walk after George Stephenson, hence linking the name of the founder of Britain's railways with the man associated with axing so many services. Even the title of Baron Beeching of East Grinstead did not make the residents feel any better towards him. The town's lower level station was served by the line from Tunbridge Wells to Three Bridges until this closed in 1967, leaving only the upper level station. This line passed through a cutting, now occupied by the A22 and named Beeching Way. The name was chosen ahead of that proposed by the locals – Beeching Cut – which was deemed politically incorrect.

Near Didcot in Oxfordshire is the village of Upton where, off Station Road, we find Beeching Close. Note how the word 'close' is pronounced as we would expect a street name to sound, yet it cannot be denied this was also intended to be seen as associated with the closures. There is another Beeching Close at Harpenden in Hertfordshire. At Maidenhatch near Pangbourne is a Beeching

Cottage. At Wallingford, Oxfordshire, off Station Road is Beeching Way. In East Sussex the town of Bexhill boasts a Beeching Road and a Beeching Park Industrial Estate.

Pubs have also seen changes, including what was The Railway in Aberystwyth, the terminus of the Cambrian Railway. As The Railway it contained a number of reminders of the resort's rail links with London and Carmarthen, both of which were axed by the man whose name is now seen outside, Lord Beeching. At Ashburton in Devon we find the Silent Whistle, a public house which casts a barely disguised swipe at the cuts which were seen as reducing employment opportunities. Aberlour in Scotland has a pub today known as the Mash Tun. Examine the title deeds and you will discover a pledge from the buyer at the time to revert the pub's name to its original one, Station Bar, should the railway station ever reopen.

30   NO RAILS

Rationalising Britain's railways did indeed see the demise of some locomotives, although not as many as one would imagine. Rolling stock suffered more but, yet again, to a lesser degree than one would expect. Jobs were lost, mostly by not replacing those who left because of retirement or a change of career. By far the biggest upheaval involved the track and the buildings.

Of the 17,830 miles of track in use, some 5,000 miles were removed. All was valuable as scrap metal, something we can only applaud in the age of recycling; even the most conservative estimate implies this would have realised 1 million tons of perfectly serviceable iron. Buildings were hit to a greater extent: no fewer than 2,363 stations and halts were boarded up, dismantled and demolished. Countless other related places experienced a similar fate, including signal boxes, sheds, and purpose-built accommodation for railway employees.

One story comes from an era not often associated with Beeching. Some buildings were utilised for other purposes, but this particular construction could not. At a time when many railway employees thought they had been robbed of their livelihood, few could have predicted that British Rail would have one of their stations stolen!

The station in question was Cleckheaton, open by 1848 and taking traffic from Heckmondwike, Low Moor and Mirfield as part of the Lancashire & Yorkshire Railway. In 1922 it was absorbed into the London & North Western Railway, into the London, Midland & Scottish the following year, and eventually it was nationalised along with the rest of the network. The last passenger train arrived here at 23.21 on 12 June 1965, with the last freight service passing through four years later.

Our interest comes from a case heard at Wakefield Crown Court on 24 April 1972. In the dock was a man from Dewsbury who was charged, as the prosecution counsel stated, with 'stealing Cleckheaton station'. It transpired that British Rail had issued a contract for the clearing of this land in August 1971. As was usual, the resulting materials and scrap would become the property of the contractors and whatever monies they gleaned from its disposal was theirs. Yet when the contractors arrived they found the work had already been done and Cleckheaton station was no more. An investigation revealed that, three weeks earlier, the man in the dock had headed the team which had been given a similar contract and had disposed of the site and its contents. This contract had been issued by another company, not British Rail who owned the property. It was decided that the defendant had acted in good faith, had not broken any laws, and was found not guilty. Furthermore, it was said he had been as much a victim as anyone else and had lost a significant amount of cash on the deal. All subsequent attempts to trace the company who had issued the contract to him failed.

Elsewhere, with the tracks and stations gone, a network of trackbeds survived which are still seen on modern Ordnance Survey maps. A few are used by heritage railways, others are overgrown and go unnoticed, and there are those which have found another use. The shallow gradient and solid base necessary for rail travel make these routes perfect for walkers and cyclists. It is probably true to say that had these old branch lines been used by as many people when they were railways as they are today, the lines would have been profitable and remained open.

Some of the buildings have survived, too. Those along the footpaths have been utilised as refreshment stops and, on some routes, cycle hire venues. Many have been adapted and are now private residences; engineering sheds still ring with the unmistakeable sound of engineers and metalworkers, now housing small businesses. Even some passenger rolling stock has found a use, making excellent museums for displaying railwayana. They have even provided unusual self-catering holiday accommodation, as indeed have the buildings.

One of the most desirable and atmospheric old railway buildings is found in Tavistock. On what was the Plymouth, Devonport & South Western Junction Railway stretch of the line to London stands Tavistock North Railway Station. The line began on paper in 1881, although it was another six years before construction work began. An estimated 2,000 navvies were employed, along with 150 horses and 7 locomotives, who together built 76 bridges, 3 tunnels, 6 viaducts, and innumerable embankments and cuttings. This took three years at a total cost of £793,000, which would equate to approximately £110 million today.

The viaduct at Tavistock alone covered five spans of 50ft each and three more of 32ft, crossing several streets. The station at Tavistock North covered around 5 acres and is the second largest on the line. The station buildings noticeably differed, with walls of granite from Dartmoor and roofs of slate from Mill Hill Quarry.

In 1968, five years after Dr Beeching's report, the station at Tavistock closed its doors to railway business. However, the stationmaster and his wife continued to live here, renaming their home Beeching's Folly! 'Snowy' Hooper, so called because of his shock of white hair, refused to believe the railway would never pass through Tavistock North again. He continued to maintain the buildings to ensure that when the next train stopped here, the disembarking passengers would find a station with clean paint, sparkling windows, and a show of flowers when the season demanded. For three years Mr Hooper steadfastly refused to believe his beloved station had closed, but the sad truth finally dawned when, in 1971, the lines were finally lifted and no trains could come here.

Sometime afterwards the Hoopers were offered the chance to purchase their home from British Rail. Delighted by the proposal, they quickly accepted. Later came the opportunity to buy the 5 acres of the goods yard, now home to the local council, which included the magnificent viaduct. Hooper declined, despite the price of just £1 sterling. Not a businessman, he failed to see the enormous profit which could have been his from the goods yard to the east, however he did understand that it would be his responsibility to pay for the repair and upkeep of the viaduct should he take up the offer.

The station is now privately owned but the rest of the property has been sold off for development, and English Heritage and the Sustrans project have taken care to ensure this colossus still dominates the skyline above the north of the town. After the track was lifted, the former trackbed became a route for walkers and cyclists, and in 1999 a private sale of the station buildings resulted in them receiving a Grade II listing.

In 2007 the buildings were purchased by the current owners, Jenny and Colin Rogers, who turned the property into three exquisite holiday cottages. It is not hard to see that the buildings were once old railway properties as they have been faithfully maintained. However, inside you will find five-star luxury accommodation fit for families of four or more.

At Ludborough in Lincolnshire we find a group of properties. Station Master's House is a large building alongside the old railway. On the tracks at the Old Station Yard, with the delightful added touch of the crossing gates still *in situ*, are three railway coaches. In truth, these are not original coaches that have been refurbished; these are reproduction carriages. Yet they are impeccable copies which have been named Audrey, Cygnus and Ibis, the names of three carriages on the Orient Express. Audrey often carried royal passengers, Ibis was the oldest of them all dating from 1925, and Cygnus was a sleeping carriage on the most famous of trains which never suffered from any of the cuts by Dr Richard Beeching.

In Cornwall near Hayle are two self-catering homes which, while they are not strictly the result of the Beeching cuts, cannot be omitted from any list. Both originate from the Ocean Mails Special train. The first is a former luggage van, which has been converted and stands in a siding at St Germans Station. This would not cater for more than a couple or a small family. The second is a former coach, which was pulled by the *City of Truro* steam locomotive between Plymouth and London Paddington on 9 May 1904 and reached 102.3mph, breaking that magical 100mph barrier – the first time such a speed had been reached by humans. The coach was the Travelling Post Office and is now also located in a siding at St Germans Station converted into a spacious self-catering holiday home.

At Wisbech St Mary an old Victorian railway carriage now offers self-catering accommodation for two or three people. However, while it is a genuine carriage, it no longer stands on an old railway line. A larger Ivywood railway carriage here has two bedrooms.

On the line which ran from Shrewsbury to Bridgnorth is Coalport Station, which closed in 1963. This former GWR station retains much of its original character and the platforms can still be seen even if most of the track is long gone. The station, which is identical in style to Arley Station on the Severn Valley Railway, is now a private residence. Also, there are two British Rail Mark I carriages, built in the 1950s, on a remaining length of track between the platforms which have been adapted to provide self-catering holiday homes for visitors.

At Dawlish Warren eight converted carriages have stood on the tracks for a number of years. With adaptations to provide wheelchair access, the coaches are named Plymouth, Exeter, Gloucester, Swindon, Newport, London, Swansea and Bristol. These names were important stops on the GWR, which also served Dawlish along the famous coastline. This site commemorates the GWR's founder, Isambard Kingdom Brunel, being named Brunel Park.

Enterprising individuals have not only thought to offer holiday homes; heritage lines frequently have themed weekends where volunteers will dress in period costume – a particular favourite being the Second World War.

Twenty years after the Beeching Report a young man named Reuben Ames came into the world. As the report's fiftieth anniversary approached, this enterprising young man turned his natural talent into a rapidly expanding and thriving business. Reuben first became interested in steam trains as a member of the 9F Club on the Bluebell Railway. Later, he became a volunteer on the Spa Valley Railway, where his duties included firing up the boiler on the steam locomotives, clipping tickets, and working in and around the station. It was when his duties brought him into contact with the public that Reuben came up with an idea.

At first he made himself a waistcoat, similar in style to those worn by employees of the Big Four railway companies prior to nationalisation in 1948. Using skills he had learned five years earlier, while working in the gentlemen's outfitting department of Marks & Spencer, he was soon sporting a hand-sewn waistcoat complete with correct buttons. Before long, his colleagues were putting in their own requests.

By the spring of 2012 a business had sprung up and Railsmart.co.uk had orders amounting to more than thirty every month. Initially, these came from the Spa Valley Railway, but soon he was supplying staff at the Epping Ongar Railway and further afield. Such numbers required a supply of reproduction railway buttons, which Reuben sourced from a supplier specialising in railway equipment. This was to prove the ideal source, with buttons bearing LMS, GWR, LNER and SR insignia. Currently, Reuben is looking to expand the range and the future of his business looks assured.

Having drawn that line across British railway history in 1963, Richard Beeching could never have envisaged his actions leading to such a new and different business venture almost half a century later.

Reproduction railway buttons for items of clothing produced by Railsmart.co.uk. (*Photographed by Reuben Ames*)

31   STATION CLOSURES

This list only includes stations closed by the Beeching Report and is not intended to be comprehensive.

Abbeyhill, Edinburgh	Closed in 1964, the station platform is still here, albeit badly overgrown.
Abbey Town, Cumbria	Closed, along with the line, in 1964.
Aberaman, South Wales	Closed in 1964.
Aberdare Low Level, South Wales	Closed in 1964; a new station was opened on the site of the old high-level station in 1988.
Aberfeldy, Perth & Kinross	Closed in 1965, the station has been demolished and a car parking area is now found here.
Aberlour, Moray	Closed in 1965, some of the station buildings remain and are used as the Speyside Way visitor centre and a tea shop.
Abermule, North Wales	Closed in 1965; nothing remains of the station today.
Aberthaw High Level, South Wales	Closed in 1964; nothing of the station can be seen today.
Abertridwr, South Wales	Closed in 1964, the buildings are long gone but the platform remains.
Ach-na-Cloich, Argyll & Bute	Closed in 1965, the platform is all that remains.
Achterneed, Highland	Closed in 1965.
Acrefair, North Wales	Closed in 1965, the site is now a small industrial estate.
Acrow Halt, Essex	Opened in 1957 to serve Acrow Engineering, it closed after just seven years.
Addingham, West Yorkshire	Closed in 1965 and demolished, now a housing estate.
Adlestrop, Gloucestershire	Closed and demolished; the stationmaster's house is a private residence and the former goods yard is home to a collection of car wrecks. The line is still open, while the station is best remembered as the title of the 1898 poem by Edward Thomas.
Advie, Highland	Closed in 1965.
Airmyn, East Yorkshire	Officially renamed Airmyn & Rawcliffe four years before it was closed, the platform still exists as the foundation for a completely new building.
Aldeburgh, Suffolk	The site of the station is now a road traffic island.

Aldridge, West Midlands	Closed on 18 January 1965, there are very real plans to reopen the station on the service between Walsall and Sutton Coldfield, with a likely through service to Birmingham New Street by 2017.
Alfreton, Derbyshire	Closed in January 1967, it reopened six years later serving both Alfreton and nearby Mansfield under the Parkway scheme, hoping to limit the number of people commuting by car. Since 1995 the station has reverted to its original name of Alfreton and serves that town alone.
Allanfearn, Highland	Closed in 1965, the station buildings survive and are now privately owned.
Alloa, Clackmannanshire	Closed in 1968, the station was reopened in 2007 and is approaching 400,000 passengers annually.
Alltddu Halt, South Wales	Closed in 1965.
Alrewas, Staffordshire	The station closed in 1965 but the track remains and is still used for freight and to divert passenger trains when engineering work on the line from Birmingham closes the line to Tamworth.
Alton Towers, Staffordshire	Closed in 1964, the station remains and is Grade II listed. The station was built on the Earl of Shrewsbury's orders as it served his estate. The station building has a three-storey tower, containing his own waiting rooms, while the platform is much longer than we would expect, again a whim of the earl who wanted to impress his many visitors. Today, the stationmaster's house and waiting room serve as holiday accommodation, while talks aimed at reintroducing a service from Stoke-on-Trent and Leek to serve the amusement park are in the early stages.
Alves, Moray	Closed in 1965.
Alyth Junction, Angus	Closed in 1967, the platforms are still here, although much of the site is waterlogged.
Amlwch, North Wales	Closed in 1964.
Andover, Hampshire	Closed in September 1964, the station was demolished and a supermarket now stands here.
Anstruther, Fife	Closed in 1965.
Apperley, West Yorkshire	Closed in 1965, talks aimed at reopening this station are well advanced and, at the time of writing, it was hoped 2014 would see passengers boarding and alighting on this line once more.
Appin, Argyll & Bute	Closed in 1966.
Arddleen, North Wales	Closed in 1965, what is known as the Station House is now a private house. This building has none of the architectural features associated with the railways and it was probably built around the same time as the nearby Montgomeryshire Canal and thus predates the railway.

Ardrossan Montgomerie Pier, Ayrshire	Closed in 1968.
Ardrossan Town, Ayrshire	Closed in 1968, it reopened in 1987 and can now boast around 20,000 passengers per year.
Ardsley, West Yorkshire	The station closed in November 1964 but not the line, and trains still pass what little is left of the station.
Armley Canal Road, West Yorkshire	The road side of the station building now doubles as commercial premises; the platform and the buildings associated with the railway have now gone.
Armley Moor, West Yorkshire	Immortalised by the Flanders & Swann song *Slow Train*, the line still comes through a place where this station used to be.
Arnage, Aberdeenshire	Closed in 1965.
Arthington, North Yorkshire	Closed in 1965, the station is now a private residence.
Arthog, Gwynedd	Closed in 1965, the story is covered in Chapter 24 on the Mawddach Trail.
Ashbury, Devon	Closed in 1966, the track was lifted soon after; the station building is now a private residence.
Ashby-de-la-Zouch, Leicestershire	Built to complement the nearby Royal Hotel, this Grade II listed building has seen at least two firm proposals for the reopening of the line, yet the chance of a train service reaching here seems as remote as ever.
Ashcott, Somerset	Closed in March 1966, freight continued to run along the line from the Eclipse Peat Company.
Ashdon Halt, Essex	Closed in September 1964, the buildings still exist, albeit in need of repair.
Ashey, Isle of Wight	Closed in 1966, it was reopened five years later as a station on the Isle of Wight Steam Railway.
Ashington, Northumberland	Closed in 1964, the line has been used for freight ever since. Recently, plans have been raised to reopen the station as part of the line from Newcastle; however, such was also on the cards in the 1990s and never got further than the planning stage.
Ashley Heath Halt, Dorset	Closed in 1964 and the track lifted, this is now part of the Castleman Trailway.
Ashley Hill, near Bristol	Closed in 1964, the trains serving Bristol still pass through here and the remains of the platform are still visible.
Ashperton, Herefordshire	Trains on the Cotswold line still pass the former site of Ashperton Station, or more correctly Ashperton Halt, as it was renamed in November 1964, five months before it closed for good.

Ashton Gate, Bristol	Followers of football will recognise this name as it is also that of the home ground of Bristol City Football Club. Indeed, the station was opened solely to serve the football ground between 1970 and 1977 (and again in 1984 for those attending the rallies of Billy Graham, the American evangelist, also at the football ground). This was by no means the first time the station had closed and reopened, since it first opened (albeit as only a platform) in 1906; it also closed in 1917 and reopened in 1926, before becoming part of the Beeching cuts in 1964. The line still carries freight and rumours of the return of passengers persist, although since 1984 they have remained rumours.
Ashwater, Devon	Closed in October 1966, the station itself is now a private residence, while the remaining buildings – a shelter and signal box – are long gone.
Ashwell, Rutland	Closed in June 1966, the line still runs through here but the station is long gone.
Athelney, Somerset	Closed in June 1964, the stationmaster's house and railwaymen's houses are still occupied. The station building itself has been moved and can be found on the playing field at Stoke St Gregory, where it acts as the pavilion for those playing cricket and tennis.
Auchengray, South Lanarkshire	Closed in 1966, nothing of the station remains today.
Auchindachy, Moray	Closed in 1968, the station and its buildings remain alongside the overgrown track.
Auchinleck, East Ayrshire	Closed in 1965, it reopened in 1984 and sees more than 35,000 passengers annually.
Auchnagatt, Aberdeenshire	Closed in 1965, the station is still largely as it was fifty years ago, albeit somewhat derelict.
Awsworth, Nottinghamshire	The last train left here in September 1964, although the station house still exists on a footpath.
Axbridge, Somerset	Closed in September 1963, the station buildings are still used as the local youth centre. This is obviously an old railway building but stands on a road today as the former trackbed has been covered by the town's bypass.
Aynho, Northamptonshire	Closed in November 1964, the line is still open and the building still in use as a private residence.
Bacup, Lancashire	Closed in 1966, there is hardly any sign of the station as the area has been redeveloped.
Back O'Loch Halt, Kirkintilloch	Closed in 1964, the site was visible until 2010 when obliterated by the new link road.
Bagillt, Flintshire	Closed in 1965.

Baguley, Greater Manchester	Closed in 1966, the line remains and there are plans to reopen a station as part of the Metrolink.
Bagworth & Elliston, Leicestershire	Closed in 1964; plans to reopen the station and line in the 1990s were shelved with the privatisation of British Rail. However, the idea remains popular and in recent years another proposal for restoring passenger services further advanced the prospect of trains returning to this area.
Bailey Gate, Dorset	Closed in March 1966, the area was redeveloped as the Bailey Gate Industrial Estate.
Baillieston, Glasgow	Closed in 1965, a new station opened in 1993 and annual passenger numbers are now approaching 100,000.
Bala, Gwynedd	Closed in 1965; following the demolition of the station, a fire station and light industry have made this their home.
Balado, Perth & Kinross	Closed in 1964, part of the platform can still be seen.
Bala Junction, Gwynedd	Closed in 1965, the buildings are long gone. This was never accessible from the road but served passengers as an interchange only.
Ballachulish, Highland	Closed in 1966.
Ballachulish Ferry, Highland	Closed in 1966, part of the platform is visible alongside the cycleway and former trackbed, albeit overgrown.
Ballater, Aberdeenshire	Closed in 1966, this was the station used by the royal family when visiting Balmoral. As a result, the old station has been maintained as a visitor centre and includes a replica of the royal carriage.
Ballifurth Farm Halt, Highland	Closed in 1965, just over six years after it opened.
Ballindalloch, Highland	Closed in 1965, although freight, in the form of whisky trains, continued for another three years. The iron lattice bridge here is now a Category A listed building.
Ballingham, Herefordshire	Closed on 2 November 1964 and the line lifted, both the platform and the station building are still here, the latter a private house.
Balquhidder, Stirling	Closed in September 1965, six weeks ahead of the planned closure in November owing to a landslide. The site is now a holiday park featuring log cabins, caravans and a camping area. The station steps, a wall and a closed-off tunnel can still be seen.
Banks, Merseyside	Closed on 7 September 1964; very little evidence remains.
Baptist End, West Midlands	Closed in 1964 and the track lifted; the trackbed and railway buildings are still there but are crumbling before the advance of nature.
Barcaldine, Argyll & Bute	Closed in 1966.

Barcombe Mills, Sussex	Closed in 1969, preservation work began in 1985 when purchased by Allan Slater. This is no heritage line but there is a station which now serves as the Wheeltappers Restaurant and Tea Room. The old stationmaster's house is a private residence, and in 2003 two cottages were built as holiday accommodation. The Lavender line could possibly extend through to Barcombe once more and in 2011 such plans included the possible construction of a new station building.
Bardney, Lincolnshire	Closing in 1970, nothing remains today, but it has not been entirely destroyed. The station building and goods shed were dismantled rather than demolished and reassembled as part of a new line under the management of Railworld in Peterborough.
Barleith, Ayrshire	Closed in 1964.
Barnard Castle, County Durham	Closed in 1965.
Barnoldswick, West Yorkshire	Almost completely demolished following closure in 1965, in its place stands a supermarket and its car park (the boundary wall was that of the coal yard); the coal yard is crossed by a road and the stationmaster's house is a private residence.
Barnwell, Northamptonshire	Closed in 1964, the stationmaster's house is still occupied as a private residence.
Barrow-on-Soar, Leicestershire	Closed in 1968, a new station opened in 1994 south-east of the original site and now carries more than 70,000 passengers per annum.
Bartlow, Cambridgeshire	Closed in 1967 and completely demolished.
Basford North, Nottinghamshire	Closed in 1964, the site is now occupied by an early and very sterile industrial estate.
Bason Bridge, Somerset	Closed in 1966 and completely demolished.
Bassenthwaite Lake, Cumbria	Closed in 1966, the station and one platform are in a bad state of repair and are virtually hidden by vegetation. The other platform and goods yard have been replaced by the A66 trunk road, while the stationmaster's house is now a private residence.
Bath Green Park, Somerset	Closed in 1966, this Grade II listed building now acts as a covered space for markets and performances.
Baynards, Surrey	Closed in 1965, it was purchased at auction in 1973 and restored to its original condition. Annual guided tours are given by the Rudgwick Preservation Society.
Bedworth, Warwickshire	The original station closed in 1965 and was demolished soon after. The present version was built in 1988 to enable locals to use the service on the line restored the previous year.

Beeston Castle & Tarporley, Cheshire	Closed in 1966, the site is in a sorry state; parts of the platform and the signal box are all that remain.
Belmont, Middlesex	Closed in 1964, the track was lifted two years later; nothing remains of the station which has now made way for a car park.
Belses, Borders	Closed in 1965.
Benderloch, Argyll & Bute	Closed in 1966.
Berkeley, Gloucestershire	Closed in 1964, the track remains to allow occasional freight through to Sharpness Docks; all buildings were demolished save for the stationmaster's house, now a private residence.
Berkeley Road, Gloucestershire	Closed in the first week of 1965, the entire site was demolished soon afterwards.
Berry Brow, West Yorkshire	Closed and demolished in 1966, the new station was opened in 2004 and now carries upwards of 25,000 passengers each year.
Berwyn, Denbighshire	Closed in 1965, the station now forms part of the Llangollen heritage railway covered in Chapter 11.
Bexhill, East Sussex	Closed in 1964, the track was lifted the following year; the station building is now home to Gorringes Auction Galleries, while the adjoining refreshment rooms have been refurbished as a pub and restaurant. While the platforms were demolished, the engine shed has been utilised as part of the small industrial estate.

Belses Station, Scottish Borders. (*Courtesy of Dr Ben Brooksbank*)

Binegar, Somerset	Closed in 1966, it was demolished to make way for a sizable private residence.
Birkenhead Woodside, Merseyside	Closed in November 1967, all that remains today is a station wall, a road bridge and a tunnel, with the land used as a bus park.
Blaby, Leicestershire	Closed in 1968, at the time of writing a preservation society are campaigning to reopen the station, having already purchased a steam locomotive to be stationed there.
Black Dog Halt, Wiltshire	Opened solely to serve Lord Lansdowne of Bowood House, who had a special compartment in one of the line's coaches, this station closed in 1965 and the buildings were demolished; it now serves as part of the National Cycle Network.
Blacksboat, Moray	Closed in 1965, the station has been restored and now stands on the Speyside Way, itself the resurfaced former trackbed.
Blackwell, Worcestershire	Closed in April 1966, much of the station has been cleared save for a few railway cottages.
Blacon, Cheshire	Closed in 1968, nothing remains of the station itself; a road bridge is the best marker for the site of the station, while a path has been laid over the old trackbed to provide a cycle and footpath.
Blaisdon, Gloucestershire	Closed in 1964 and demolished.
Blandford Forum, Dorset	Closed in 1964, the site of the station is now a housing estate.
Bleadon & Uphill, Somerset	Closed in 1964, the buildings were first used to house a small museum. This later closed and the exhibits relocated, leaving the platform and the stationmaster's house as the only remaining evidence.
Bletchington, Oxfordshire	Closed in 1964, the station building and the land around are now home to an industrial estate.
Bloxwich, West Midlands	Closed in 1965, a new station opened on the line north of the original in 1989.
Blyth, Northumberland	Closed in 1964, the buildings were derelict by the time they were demolished in 1972; the stationmaster's house is the only surviving part, now serving as a private residence. In 1999 a proposal to reopen a station at Blyth was shelved until raised again in 2009.
Boat of Garten, Highland	Closed in 1966, the line was opened as a heritage railway in 1998.
Bodmin General, Cornwall	Closed in 1963, the station is currently used as the headquarters of the Bodmin & Wenford Railway heritage line.

Bodmin North, Cornwall	The line closed in 1967, the station was later demolished and a supermarket now occupies this site.
Bogside, Ayrshire	Closed in 1967.
Bolton Abbey, North Yorkshire	Closed in 1965, it reopened thirty-three years later when the buildings were restored and a passenger service resumed.
Bonnybridge Halt, Falkirk	Closed in 1967.
Bont Newydd, Gwynedd	Closed in 1965, little evidence of the site remains save for the stationmaster's house which is now a private residence.
Bonwm Halt, Denbighshire	Closed in 1964, a few wooden platform supports mark the location, and while the line is being rebuilt by the Llangollen Railway Company, this halt is not part of their current plans.
Borrowash, Derbyshire	The last passenger train left here in 1966; much of the station was demolished in 1984, but the original station building is now a private house. A flight of steps leading to the lower platform can still be made out.
Botanic Gardens, East Yorkshire	Closed in 1964, the site has been developed into the Old Zoological public house and its adjoining car park.
Brackley Central, Northamptonshire	Closed in 1965, the station building is now home to a tyre company, while much of the site contains industrial units.
Bradford Peverell, Dorset	Closed in 1966, there is a possibility of this reopening as a halt.
Bradwell, Buckinghamshire	Closed in 1964, the trackbed is now part of the Milton Keynes Redway System; this cycle path passes the platforms but the station buildings were demolished long ago.
Braithwaite, Cumbria	Closed in April 1966, the only remaining evidence is the station building, now a private residence.
Bramber, West Sussex	Closed in 1966, the trackbed is now part of the Downs Link footpath, while the station area is occupied by a traffic island and Bramber Garden Nursery. A visit to the garden centre may not be high on the agenda of railway enthusiasts; however, a station name sign is found inside – a particularly fine wooden example with hand-carved lettering.
Bramley & Wonersh, Surrey	Closed in 1965, with the station demolished shortly afterwards, the overgrown trackbed became part of the Downs Link footpath and cycleway in the 1980s. Along with other stations on the former Cranleigh line, this is one of the stations marked for possible reopening.
Breamore, Hampshire	Closed in May 1964, the station building still exists, although the trackbed, while still evident, is overgrown.
Bredon, Gloucestershire	Closed in 1965, nothing of the station remains.

Brent, Devon	Closed in 1964, the station was soon demolished; the signal box and goods shed on the westbound line are still standing.
Bridge of Allan, Stirling	Closed in 1965, the station buildings have been used for residential accommodation. A new station to the south of the original site was built in 1985 and now serves a quarter of a million passengers annually.
Bridge of Dun, Aberdeenshire	Closed in 1967, the station reopened twenty-six years later.
Bridgeton, Glasgow	Closed in 1964, the line reopened in 1979 and has seen a steady increase in passenger numbers, now approaching half a million annually.
Brightlingsea, Essex	Closed in 1964 and demolished five years later in November 1969.
Brimscombe, Gloucestershire	Closed in November 1964, the station has all but disappeared.
Briton Ferry, South Wales	Closed in 1964, the present station was reopened on the South Wales main line in 1994 and now carries upwards of 30,000 passengers a year.
Brixham, Devon	A branch line from Churston, still the passing loop on the Paignton & Dartmouth heritage line, this station was ostensibly to serve the fishing port which closed in 1963. Suggestions for reopening the branch may come to fruition considering the gaps which now exist on the line.
Broadclyst, Devon	Closed in 1966, the line, station building and goods shed survive and in recent years there has been talk of reopening the station, for an estate of some 3,000 homes now exists here.
Broadstone, Dorset	Closed in March 1966, the site is now occupied by the Broadstone Leisure Centre, a car park and a traffic roundabout, with a new housing development to the north crossing the former trackbed.
Bronwydd Arms, Carmarthenshire	Closed in 1965, everything was demolished except for the platform. When the station reopened in 1978, various buildings were recovered from other parts of the line to bring this station back to life as part of the Gwili Railway heritage line, covered in Chapter 15.
Brookland, Kent	The line closed in 1967 and the station building is now a private residence; both platforms are very overgrown, but the track survives. Level crossings at either end of the station are operated by the crew of those trains bringing nuclear waste from Dungeness Nuclear Power Station.
Brownhills, West Midlands	The station, along with its passenger traffic, ended in 1965, yet goods traffic continued until the end of 1983 and the line was not lifted until 1985.

Brucklay, Aberdeenshire	Closed in 1965.
Brynkir, Gwynedd	Closed in 1964.
Buckingham, Buckinghamshire	Closed to passengers in 1964 and freight two years later, the only visible remains of the station are the platform edges, themselves rapidly becoming unrecognisable as they weather away. The trackbed has been filled in and is now a woodland walk.
Bude, Cornwall	Closed in 1965, the site is now occupied by an early housing development. The cycle path is not, as is often said, on the line of the trackbed, but runs roughly parallel to it. Look carefully and a single pillar from the former station entranceway can be found at the centre of a mass of ivy. Further along, the railway bridge over the River Neet is still intact.
Budleigh Salterton, Devon	Closed in 1967, nothing remains of the station, which was bulldozed to make way for a modern housing estate.

Bude Station and yard in April 1964. (*Courtesy of Dr Ben Brooksbank*)

Buntingford, Hertfordshire	Closed in 1964, at the time of writing the station building is undergoing refurbishment.
Burlescombe, Somerset	Closed in October 1964, few signs of its existence remain.
Burslem, Staffordshire	Closed in 1964, no sign of the station remains; it has been landscaped as a park.
Burton Constable, East Yorkshire	Closed in 1964, very little of the original station remains.
Cadishead, Greater Manchester	Closed in November 1964, the station is still there, albeit in a sorry state and badly overgrown.
Caernarvon, Caernarvonshire	Closed in 1970.
Cairnbulg, Aberdeenshire	Closed in 1965.
Callander, Stirling	Closed in 1965, the site is now a car park, although part of the platform can still be seen.
Callington, Cornwall	Closed in November 1966, little remains today.
Calne, Wiltshire	Closed in 1965, the station buildings were a target for vandals until they were demolished to make way for the Station Road Industrial Estate.
Camelford, Cornwall	Closed in 1966, the station building is now a private residence with the site also housing a cycle museum.
Cannock, Staffordshire	Closed in 1965 and reopened in 1989, a small section of the southbound platform remains to the north of the new platform.
Caradog Falls Halt, Ceredigion	This station was closed in 1964 because of flood damage, two months before the official closure.
Carcroft & Adwick-le-Street, South Yorkshire	Originally known as Adwick when it opened in 1866, it became Carcroft & Adwick-le-Street in 1880. Closing in 1967, the station reopened in October 1993, albeit on a new site south-east of the original; it is now known as Adwick Station once more.
Carmyle, Glasgow	Closed in 1964, the station reopened in 1993 and now handles well over 120,000 passengers each year.
Carno, Powys	Closed in 1965, from 2009 the Welsh Assembly lobbied to investigate the reopening of this station.
Carnwath, Lothian	Closed in 1966.
Carrog, Denbighshire	Closed in 1964, it was reopened in 1996 and is the current terminus for the Llangollen heritage railway line.
Castle Ashby & Earls Barton, Northamptonshire	Closed in 1964, the station buildings now house a restaurant by the name of Dunkley's, which also features two former railway carriages.
Castlethorpe, Buckinghamshire	Closed in 1964, the buildings were demolished soon afterwards, although the platforms and line remain and trains continue to run through here. Campaigns have been run to reopen the station to passengers.

Cattistock, Dorset	Closed in 1966, little evidence remains of this halt.
Cavendish, Suffolk	Closing in 1967, there is little evidence remaining.
Chacewater, Cornwall	Closed to passenger traffic in 1963, the station served goods traffic for Blue Circle Cement for many years afterwards; the station building and its platform still exist.
Challow, Oxfordshire	Closed in 1964, little of the original buildings and platforms survives.
Chard, Somerset	Closed in 1966, several attempts to close and reopen the station have yet to prove decisive. A support group continue to campaign for the reopening.
Charfield, Gloucestershire	Closed in 1965, the station building and stationmaster's house are now private homes.
Chatteris, Cambridgeshire	Closed in 1967, the station was demolished soon afterwards, while the trackbed was utilised for the new A141 trunk road.
Cheadle, Staffordshire	Closed in 1963, the stationmaster's house still stands as a private residence; the remains of the station were cleared for a new housing development in 1994.
Cheadle Heath, Greater Manchester	Closed in early 1967, a single line is still used by freight trains bringing limestone quarried in the Peak District; the station and its buildings were demolished to accommodate a Morrisons supermarket and its car park.
Cheddar, Somerset	Closed to passenger traffic in 1963, the main buildings of the station are occupied as office units; the removal of the overhanging roof makes it look less like a former station.
Cheddleton, Staffordshire	Closed in 1965, it was saved from demolition in 1974 when local businessman Norman Hancock stopped his large vehicle on the level crossing. A successful local campaign saved the building, which was eventually given a Grade II listing. The line reopened thirty years after its original closure as part of the Churnet Valley heritage line.
Cheltenham Spa Malvern Road, Gloucestershire	Closed in January 1966, the site was levelled by the early 1970s. It remains undeveloped and the Gloucestershire & Warwickshire heritage railway desire an extension to Cheltenham Spa Lansdown Road, through the Malvern Road site, linking to the cross-country route; this remains an attainable goal.
Chilcompton, Someset	Closed in 1966, the station is somewhat overgrown today but will benefit from the work of the Somerset & Dorset Railway Heritage Trust, who continue to work to reopen the line.
Chittering, Bristol	Opened in 1917 to serve a large munitions factory, it was abandoned shortly after the First World War; it did, however, serve employees on the Chittering Trading Estate until its closure in 1964.

Chorlton-cum-Hardy, Cheshire	Closed in 1967 but reopened as part of the Metrolink in July 2011.
Christian Malford Halt, Wiltshire	Closed in 1965, nothing survives but the access path to the platform.
Churchdown, Gloucestershire	Closed in 1964, the station has all but disappeared, although Station Close is a lasting reminder.
Churchtown, Lancashire	Closed in 1964, the bridge and embankments were removed the following year. Suggestions that this was to prevent any U-turn on the decision to close the line have never been proven.
Churston, Devon	As with other stations on the line, it never actually closed but saw ownership transferred to the Paignton & Dartmouth Steam Railway heritage line in 1972.
Chwilog, Powys	Closed in 1964, the platform is still here, as is the stationmaster's house; the rest of the site is covered by a new housing development and a bus station.
Clare, Suffolk	Closed in 1967, the station building and platform are still evident and are kept in good condition, although the platform does have a fair amount of ivy clinging to it.
Clay Cross, Derbyshire	Closed in 1967, there is no sign of any remains; talk of reopening remains only talk.
Clayton Bridge, Greater Manchester	Closed in October 1968, nothing remains of the station, platform or signal box, but the level crossings are still operational remotely.
Cleckheaton, Yorkshire	Closed in 1965, the story of 'the theft of Cleckheaton Station' is covered in Chapter 30.
Clifton Bridge, Bristol	Closed in 1964, the line remains open and something of the platforms can still be made out beneath the ivy.
Clough Fould, Lancashire	Closed in 1966.
Coalville Town, Leicestershire	Closed in 1964, one of the station buildings still stands, occupied by a children's nursery.
Cobbinshaw, South Lanarkshire	Closed in 1964, nothing of the station remains.
Cobridge, Staffordshire	Closed in 1964, the trackbed is a footpath and the tunnel filled in.
Cockermouth, Cumbria	Closed in 1966, the station has been demolished and the Cockermouth Mountain Rescue and Cumbria Fire Service Headquarters now occupy the site.
Cole, Somerset	Closed in 1966.
Collingham, South Yorkshire	Closed in 1965, the site of the station is now buried under a road, while its coal yard is a car park.

Colnbrook, Middlesex	Closed in 1965, the station is now a private residence; the remaining buildings were demolished several years after closure. While the track has been lifted, the route remains a viable option for part of the proposed Heathrow Airtrack link.
Colnbrook Estate Halt, Middlesex	Closed in 1965, the station buildings were demolished, but the line continues to serve depots for fuel and aggregate on the industrial estate.
Combpyne, Devon	Closed in 1965, the station house is all that remains.
Congresbury, Somerset	Both line and station closed in 1963 and the buildings were demolished soon afterwards; the platforms can still be made out as walkers and cyclists pass through along the Strawberry Line Trail.
Cononley, South Yorkshire	Closed in March 1965, the station reopened in 1988 and now sees over 100,000 passengers a year.
Consall, Staffordshire	Closed in 1965, the station reopened in 1998 on the Churnet Valley heritage line.
Corby, Northamptonshire	Closed in 1966, but briefly reopened between 1987 and 1990, the modern station has been open to passengers since February 2009 and saw over 175,000 rail users in 2011. During its days of closure Corby was oddly proud of being the largest town in the country (and the third largest in Europe) to be without a railway service.
Corsham, Wiltshire	Closed to passengers in 1965, two years after freight, the goods shed is still standing, while the old footbridge still allows pedestrians to cross the main line.
Corwen, Denbighshire	Closed in 1964, the Llangollen Railway heritage line is currently constructing an extension to bring trains back to the town.
Cotherstone, County Durham	Closed in November 1964, the station building is now a private house; the platforms remain visible.
Cound Halt, Shropshire	Closed in September 1963, many believe it was earmarked for closure even before the report was planned.
Coundon Road, West Midlands	Closed in 1965, the original signal box (dating from 1876) remained in service until 2009 when it was automated.
Cowes, Isle of Wight	Closed in 1966, the site has been demolished and a supermarket built in its place.
Cranleigh, Surrey	Closed in 1965 when the site was demolished, it is now buried beneath the Stocklund Square housing and shopping centre development.
Crawford, South Lanarkshire	Closed in 1965.
Creagan, Argyll & Bute	Closed in 1966.

Cranleigh, Surrey, from the bridge. (*Courtesy of Dr Ben Brooksbank*)

Creekmoor Halt, Dorset	Closed in 1966, the site was demolished and any remaining evidence is now buried under the A349 road.
Crianlarich, Stirling	Closed in 1965, the site was a lumber yard for a while; the station building now houses the Crianlarich Community Centre.
Crieff, Perth & Kinross	Closed in 1964.
Cromland, Highland	Closed in 1965.
Crossens, Merseyside	Closed in 1964.
Crosshouse, Ayrshire	Closed in 1966.
Culcheth, Lancashire	Closed in 1964, a rear wall of one of the platforms continues to be used as part of a building.
Culter, Aberdeenshire	Closed in 1966, some of the bridges and the platform are still visible along the rail trail.
Cumnock, Ayrshire	Closed in 1965, the line remains open to this day.
Cutnall Green Halt, Worcestershire	Closed in 1965.
Cynwyd, Denbighshire	Closed in 1964 due to flooding, two months prior to the official closure date.
Daggons Road, Dorset	Closed in 1964, the only sign of the railway today is the cul-de-sac named Station Yard.

Daimler Halt, West Midlands	Closed in 1965, this station was never open to the general public but solely for the use of the workers at the Daimler factory.
Dalcross, Highland	Closed in 1965, most of the buildings and platform are still visible.
Darby End, West Midlands	Closed in 1964.
Darfield, South Yorkshire	The station closed in 1963, but the line remained open until 1988 when subsidence became a problem.
Darlaston James Bridge, West Midlands	Closed in 1965, nothing remains of the station today, although the lines are still in use.
Darley Dale, Derbyshire	Closed in 1965, it is now part of the Peak Rail line.
Dauntsey, Wiltshire	Closed in 1965, most of the station was demolished; one platform and the station house are now used as private accommodation, while the station canopy was moved to Yatton.
Dava, Highland	Closed in 1964, the station building, platforms and stationmaster's house are still there.
Denstone, Staffordshire	Closed in 1965.
Derby Friargate, Derbyshire	Closed in 1964, all that remains is the bridge built by Andrew Handyside & Co. and the adjacent staircase to the central platform.
Derby Nottingham Road, Derbyshire	Closed in 1967.
Desborough, Northamptonshire	Closed in 1968.
Desford, Leicestershire	Closed in 1964, the line is all that remains, now used solely for freight.
Devizes, Wiltshire	Closed in 1966, the growth of the town has brought about talk of reopening the station, although little of the land remains having been sold off for development.
Devonport Kings Road, Devon	Closed in 1964, City College Plymouth was built on the site.
Didsbury, Cheshire	Closed in 1967, the station reopens in 2013 as part of the Metrolink system.
Diggle, Greater Manchester	Closed in 1968, little remains of the station, although the signal box is still operational.
Dolgellau, Gwynedd	Closed in 1965, it is now the eastern end of the Mawddach Trail, covered in Chapter 24; the station site is buried under the Dolgellau bypass.
Dornock, Dumfries & Galloway	Closed in 1965.
Doune, Stirling	Closed in 1965, the station house remains as part of a new housing development.

Downton, Wiltshire	Closed in 1964, the station site has been developed as a residential estate.
Draycott, Somerset	Closed in 1963, the station building is now a private residence.
Draycott & Breaston, Derbyshire	Closed in 1966.
Dreghorn, Ayrshire	Closed in 1964.
Dronfield, Derbyshire	Closed in 1967, the station reopened in 1981 and passenger numbers have increased steadily ever since.
Droylsden, Greater Manchester	Closed in 1968.
Drws-y-Nant, Gwynedd	Closed in 1965, the station remained unchanged for more than twenty years, by which time it was derelict; it was then levelled to make way for road improvements.
Drybridge, Ayrshire	Closed in 1969, the station building is now a private residence.
Dudley, West Midlands	Closed in 1964, the buildings were demolished three years later and the first freightliner terminal in the country was constructed on the site.
Dunball, Somerset	Closed in 1964, nothing of the station remains today.
Duncraig, Highland	Closed in 1964, the station reopened in 1976 and the number of passengers has now reached around 500 per annum.
Dunlop, East Ayrshire	Closed in June 1966, it reopened nine months later and now handles more than 80,000 passengers annually.
Dunmere Halt, Cornwall	Closed in 1964, the platform remains and the trackbed has been made into a footpath.
Dunphail, Perth	Closed in 1964, the platforms, buffers, station building and stationmaster's house remain.
Dunrobin Castle, Highland	Closed in 1965, it reopened in 1985 and now serves 500 passengers each year.
Dunsbear Halt, Devon	Closed in 1965, it now forms part of the Tarka Trail.
Dunstable North, Bedfordshire	Closed in 1965, the buildings were subsequently demolished and it is now the site of the South Bedfordshire District Council offices.
Dunstable Town, Bedfordshire	Closed in 1965, it was dismantled in stages; the region was used predominantly as a car park from the 1990s until the whole area was redeveloped as a housing estate in 2008.
Duror, Highland	Closed in 1966.
Durston, Somerset	Closed in 1964, all that remains today is the Station Hotel and evidence of the trackbed.
Dyce, Aberdeenshire	Closed in 1965, it reopened in 1984 and around half a million passengers now pass through here annually.

Earswick, North Yorkshire	Closed in 1965, the site has been redeveloped as the Flag and Whistle public house.
East Budleigh, Devon	Closed in 1967, the station buildings are now private residences.
East Langton, Leicestershire	Closed in 1968; while everything disappeared years ago, the outline of the buildings can still be made out.
East Leake, Nottinghamshire	Closed in 1969, the central platform remains and it is likely the station will reopen as part of the Great Central Railway heritage line.
East Linton, East Lothian	Closed in 1964, plans to reopen the station have been tabled before the Scottish Parliament.
Eckington, Worcestershire	Closed in 1965.
Edinburgh Princes Street, Edinburgh	Closed in 1964, the station was soon demolished. The Caledonian Hotel remains open and a major office development was constructed on the site of the parcels office in the 1990s.
Edington, Somerset	Closed in 1966.
Eglinton Street, Glasgow	Closed in 1965, the platforms and access towers to those platforms are still visible.
Egloskerry, Cornwall	Closed in 1966, the former station building is now a bed and breakfast establishment.
Elderslie, Renfrewshire	Closed in 1966, the station was demolished soon afterwards and the only remaining evidence is the bricked-up entrance.
Elland, West Yorkshire	Closed in 1962, the viaduct and signal box remain and although plans to reopen the station in 2000 failed because of financing, there seems every chance of a working station here again sooner rather than later.
Ellon, Aberdeenshire	Closed in 1965.
Elswick, Northumberland	Closed in 1962, the buildings were demolished. Later track realignment removed all traces of the station.
Embsay, North Yorkshire	Closed in 1965, it was reopened in 1981 by the Yorkshire Dales Railway. In 2004 the ITV soap *Emmerdale* used the station as the fictional Hotten Station.
Euxton Balshaw Lane, Lancashire	Closed in 1969 and reopened in 1998.
Evercreech, Somerset	Closed in 1966, the station buildings are private homes and the former goods yard is now an industrial estate.
Evercreech New, Somerset	Closed in 1966.
Evershot, Dorset	Closed in 1966, a few signs remain near the tunnel entrance.

Exminster, Devon	Closed in 1964, the station building still stands; the signal box was removed and is preserved at Broadway, Worcestershire.
Eye, Suffolk	Closed to passengers in 1931 and finally to goods in 1964.
Fakenham, Norfolk	Closed in 1964, it is a potential site for the Mid-Norfolk Railway, but it will require a complete new building as sheltered housing now occupies the original site.
Falkirk Camelon, Falkirk	Closed in 1967, a new and much larger station opened in 1994 and now handles around 100,000 passengers each year.
Falls of Cruachan, Argyll & Bute	Closed in 1965, a new station opened in 1988 and handles around 200 passengers per annum.
Fawley, Herefordshire	Closed in 1964, the site is now the garden of a private residence.
Featherstone, West Yorkshire	Closed in 1967 and demolished, there is a new station here today, which opened in 1992.
Fenny Compton, Warwickshire	Closed in 1964, much of the track remains, although all signs of the station buildings have long disappeared.
Fernhill Heath, Worcestershire	Closed in 1965, the site of the station is marked by the footbridge only, itself not part of the original station.
Fishguard & Goodwick, Pembrokeshire	Closed in 1964, it reopened in 2012 and now sees seven trains per day during the week.
Fishponds, Bristol	Closed in 1966, most of the station buildings were demolished the following year; some signs remain, as those travelling the Bristol and Bath Railway Path will see. Note the path detours from the original route slightly as the supermarket car park has encroached.
Fitzwilliam, North Yorkshire	Closed in 1967, a new station opened in 1982 a short distance north of the site of the original.
Flax Bourton, Somerset	Closed in 1964; there were effectively two stations and each has seen a very different life since closure. The first station footbridge remains, as does the station building, now a private residence. The second station is much as it was left, although time has not been kind and it is boarded up and slowly falling apart.
Fleetwood, Lancashire	Closed in 1966.
Foleshill, Warwickshire	Closed in 1964, the line is still operational but there are few signs of the old station other than the platform.
Fordingbridge, Hampshire	Closed in 1964, the station site has been redeveloped; however, the approaching road retains its original name of Station Road.
Forest Row, East Sussex	Closed in 1967, parts of the platforms can still be seen, as can the goods shed among industrial units.

Fowey, Cornwall	Closed in 1965, the site is now occupied by a car park, but some of the railway buildings still stand.
Fraserburgh, Aberdeenshire	Closed in 1965.
Fritwell & Somerton, Oxfordshire	Closed in 1964.
Frizinghall, West Yorkshire	Closed in 1965, the station reopened twenty-two years later. With the original station long gone, a new station was built with the northbound platform occupying almost exactly the same place; the opposite platform is the other side of the Frizinghall Road.
Fyling Hall, North Yorkshire	Closed in 1965, the station is on the Cinder Track and the platforms remain, albeit overgrown.
Gaerwen, Anglesey	Closed in 1966, the signal box is still operational.
Gailes, Ayrshire	Closed in 1967, the station's level crossing is still operational.
Galashiels, Scotland	Closed in 1969.
Garneddwen Halt, Gwynedd	Closed in 1965, the platforms are still visible.
Gateshead, Ayrshire	Closed in 1969, the single platform is still intact, albeit overgrown.
Gilbey's Cottages Halt, Moray	Closed in 1965.
Glan Conwy, North Wales	Closed in 1964, it reopened in 1970 as the Conwy & Llanrwst Station; it was renamed Glan Conwy ten years later and now sees about 2,500 passengers annually.
Glan Llyn Halt, Gwynedd	Closed in 1965, the station is now used by the Bala Lake Railway as the grotto on their Santa Specials.
Glasgow Cross, Glasgow	Closed in 1965, rumours of a possible reopening persist.
Glastonbury & Street, Somerset	Closed in 1965, the site is now occupied by a timber yard. The level crossing gates at the entrance are replicas and the canopy from the railway station now serves as a shelter for the market at Glastonbury.
Glemsford, Suffolk	Closed in 1967.
Glen Parva, Leicestershire	Closed in 1968.
Glyndyfrdwy, Denbighshire	Closed in 1964 due to flood damage, two months before the official closure date. It reopened in 1993 as part of the Llangollen Railway heritage line.
Golcar, West Yorkshire	Closed in 1965.
Gollanfield, Highland	Closed in 1965.
Gorebridge, Midlothian	Closed in 1969, the station is in line for reopening as part of the future Waverley line.

Grampound, Cornwall	Closed in 1964, the site of two platforms and two railway cottages is still visible from passing trains.
Grange Court, Gloucestershire	Closed in 1964, the station and its buildings were demolished.
Grange Road, West Sussex	Closed in 1976, the station was bulldozed and redeveloped as a medical centre and row of shops with accommodation above.
Grantown-on-Spey, Perth & Kinross	Closed in 1965, the site has been flattened with the exception of the stationmaster's house; reopening is planned as part of the Rails to Grantown project.
Great Bridge North, West Midlands	Closed in 1964, the station and its yard gradually disappeared and nothing remains today.
Great Bridge South, West Midlands	Closed in 1964.
Great Linford, Buckinghamshire	Closed in 1967, the building was demolished but the platforms remain and are visible from the trackbed, now the Milton Keynes Redway System, a cycleway.
Greatstone-on-Sea, Kent	Closed in 1967, the concrete area is now a car park and while the trackbed can still be traced, the rest of the station has been demolished.
Great Wyrley & Cheslyn Hay, Staffordshire	Closed in 1965, both platforms can still be seen; the rest of the site has been developed into a housing estate.
Gretna Green, Dumfries & Galloway	Closed in 1965, a new station opened in 1993, just west of the original, and now carries some 30,000 passengers annually.
Gretton, Northamptonshire	Closed in 1965, the platforms remain; the station buildings are privately owned.
Grimstone & Frampton, Dorset	Closed in 1966, the station was quickly demolished and is now home to the Minster Fuels depot.
Groeslon, Gwynedd	Closed in 1964.
Grogley Halt, Cornwall	Closed in 1967.
Guisborough, North Yorkshire	Closed in 1964.
Gwinear Road, Cornwall	Closed in 1962, the down platform is still very much intact.
Hailsham, East Sussex	Closed in 1968.
Halton, Lancashire	Closed in 1966, the trackbed remains as a way for cyclists and walkers.
Halwill Junction, Devon	Closed in 1966, the housing development here includes a Beeching Close. In 1990 an area of almost 3 hectares was purchased by Devon Wildlife Trust and a nature reserve was created, eventually crossed by a cycleway along part of the old trackbed.

Ham Green, Somerset	Closed in 1964.
Hammerwich, Staffordshire	Closed in 1965, the trackbed is still obvious and the footbridge still stands.
Hanley, Staffordshire	Closed in 1964, the station has been demolished and the cutting refilled; it is now home to a car park.
Harburn, Edinburgh	Closed in 1964, nothing of the station remains.
Haresfield, Gloucestershire	Closed in 1965, the realigned tracks have eradicated all signs of the station.
Harpenden, Hertfordshire	Closed in 1965, all signs of the station have been covered by a housing development.
Hartfield, East Sussex	Closed in 1967, the station buildings are occupied by a private residence and a day nursery, while the track is now the Forest Way cycle path.
Hatherleigh, Devon	Closed in 1965.
Havenstreet, Isle of Wight	Closed in 1966, it reopened in 1971 as part of the Isle of Wight Steam Railway.
Haverhill, Suffolk	Closed in 1967.
Hawkhead, Renfrewshire	Closed in 1966, a new station opened in 1991 and now handles 150,000 passengers annually.
Hawsker, North Yorkshire	Closed in 1965, it is now home to Trailways Cycle Hire on the Cinder Track.
Hayburn Wyke, North Yorkshire	Closed in 1965, it is on the Cinder Track.
Heapey, Lancashire	Closed by the Beeching Report in 1966; by this time it was used for freight only, as the last passenger service had come through in January 1960.
Heathfield, East Sussex	Closed in 1965, the station site is now an industrial estate and car park, while the trackbed has been resurfaced as part of the Cuckoo Trail.
Hednesford, Staffordshire	Closed in 1965, it reopened twenty-four years later and now sees around 150,000 passengers a year.
Hedon, East Yorkshire	Closed in 1964, the station building is now a private residence; the platform is also clearly visible.
Heeley, South Yorkshire	Closed in 1968, the line is still operational, running underneath two large bridges which are all that remain of the station.
Hele & Bradninch, Devon	Closed in 1964, the station buildings, although mainly empty, are still recognisable; the former goods shed is home to a small engineering company.
Hellingly, East Sussex	Closed in 1965, the station building is now a private residence and is passed by the Cuckoo Trail footpath and cycleway along the former trackbed.

Helmshore, Lancashire	Closed in 1966, the abandoned part of the railway has been replaced by the Station Road development, with the signal box now a private residence.
Helpston, Cambridgeshire	Closed in 1966, the goods shed, signal box and level crossings survive.
Helston, Cornwall	Closed in 1962, all that remains is the former goods shed which has been converted into a private house and a granite wall. The remainder was demolished and a housing estate now stands here.
Henbury, Bristol	Closed in 1964, there are plans to reopen the station as part of the Greater Bristol Metro scheme.
Henfield, West Sussex	Closed in 1966, the former trackbed forms part of the Downs Link footpath. The area has been developed as the Beechings Estate and includes Station Road.
Henstridge, Somerset	Closed in 1966, only a road bridge north of the former station helps to mark its location.
Hesketh Bank, Lancashire	Closed in 1964, with little evidence remaining.
Hesketh Park, Lancashire	As with Hesketh Bank.
Highlandman, Perth & Kinross	Closed in 1964.
Hindley South, Greater Manchester	Closed in 1964, nothing remains of the station today.
Hole, Devon	Closed in 1965.
Holme Hale, Norfolk	Closed in 1964.
Holme Lacy, Herefordshire	Closed in 1964, the station buildings were demolished long ago, although the platforms still exist and are overgrown.
Holmsley, Hampshire	Closed in 1964, the road now occupies some of the trackbed; some remnants of the platforms can still be seen, while the station house is a tea room.
Holsworthy, Cornwall	Closed in 1966, part of the trackbed has been resurfaced as the Ruby Way, part of the National Cycle Network. The station buildings were demolished long ago.
Holt, Norfolk	Closed in 1964, talks are in the early stages regarding reopening this as part of the Norfolk Orbital Railway.
Holt Junction, Wiltshire	Closed in 1966, all evidence of the station was swept away by 1970.
Horam, East Sussex	Closed in 1965, little evidence can be seen of the station buildings today, although the line is now part of the Cuckoo Trail footpath and cycleway.
Horfield, Bristol	Closed in 1964, campaigners continue to call for the station to be reopened.

Hornsea Bridge, East Yorkshire	Closed in 1964, the station was demolished; a new road scheme can be seen alongside an industrial estate which was formerly the goods yard.
Hornsea Town, East Yorkshire	Closed in 1964.
Horsebridge, Hampshire	Closed in 1964, the site became increasingly derelict until it was restored by Hampshire County Council. The trackbed is now the Test Way footpath and the station has been converted into a residential property, with a carriage moved in to act as the dining room.
Horwich, Lancashire	Closed in 1965, the site was demolished and is now a public park.
Hoy, Highland	Closed in 1965.
Humberstone Road, Leicestershire	Closed in 1968, nothing of the station remains save for the station building. However, it is no longer found here: as a listed building it was transported to the Battlefield Line heritage railway as Shenton Station.
Hurstbourne, Hampshire	Closed in 1964, the site was cleared and is now home to a scrap metal dealer.
Hutton Gate, North Yorkshire	Closed in 1964, all that remains is the station building, now a private house.
Ilkeston North, Derbyshire	Closed in 1964, the bridges have been filled in and the station buildings cleared. The police station was built on the site in the 1990s, while part of the trackbed forms something of the Cotmanhay Linear Park.
Imperial Colleges Halt, Moray	Closed in 1965.
Irthlingborough, Northamptonshire	Closed in 1964.
Isfield, East Sussex	Closed in 1969, the station is now part of the Lavender line heritage railway.
Kegworth, Nottinghamshire	Closed in 1968, the station house and the goods shed are all that remain.
Kelvinbridge, Glasgow	Closed in 1964, the station building was destroyed by fire in 1968.
Kelvin Hall, Glasgow	Closed in 1964, the station was used as a workshop and an auction house until, after lying empty for many years, it was demolished in 2007. The goods yard was occupied by a scrap metal dealer for some time.
Kenilworth, Warwickshire	Closed in 1965, a new station is planned and is hoped to be open in 2013.
Kentallen, Highland	Closed in 1966.
Ketton & Collyweston, Rutland	Closed in 1966, the line is still used but the station buildings are long gone.

Keyingham, East Yorkshire	Closed in 1964, the station buildings are now a private residence.
Kibworth, Leicestershire	Closed in 1968, it was occupied by a company selling fencing and timber for a while. Around this time the former station car park became home to new housing.
Kidlington, Oxfordshire	Closed in 1964, the station buildings have been home to a printing business, a plastics company, an antique shop, and even a company repairing dentures. The goods yard later became an industrial estate known as Station Field.
Kidsgrove Liverpool Road, Staffordshire	Closed in 1964, the station is long gone and the site is now occupied by a supermarket.
Kilbarchan, Renfrewshire	Closed in 1966, much of the platform remains and the trackbed now forms part of National Cycle Network Route 7.
Kilbirnie, Ayrshire	Closed in 1966, the island platform is still visible, while the trackbed forms part of National Cycle Network Route 7.
Kildwick & Crosshills, North Yorkshire	Closed in 1965, the buildings have been demolished while the goods yard is used by the local council department responsible for road repairs.
Killin, Stirling	Closed in 1965, the last passenger train was seen at the end of September – five weeks before the official closure date – owing to a landslide at Glen Ogle.
Kilmaurs, Ayrshire	Closed in 1966, the station reopened in 1984 and now handles more than 80,000 passengers each year.
Kimberley East, Nottinghamshire	Closed in 1964, the buildings are now occupied by small commercial concerns; the trackbed is used by walkers and horse riders even though no official pathway exists.
Kinaldie, Aberdeenshire	Closed in 1964.
King's Cliffe, Northamptonshire	Closed in 1966, nothing remains.
Kingshouse, Stirling	Closed in 1965, the station effectively served the Kingshouse Hotel – the only local building of any note.
Kingskerswell, Devon	Closed in 1964, the line still runs through and the platforms are still clearly visible.
Kingsley & Froghall, Staffordshire	Closed in 1965, it reopened as part of the Churnet Valley heritage railway in 2001.
Kingsnowe, Edinburgh	Closed in 1964, the station reopened in 1974 and now handles 20,000 passengers annually.
Kintore, Aberdeenshire	Closed in 1964, proposals to reopen the station were tabled in 2010.
Kiplingcotes, East Yorkshire	Closed in 1965, the platforms, station buildings and signal box remain seemingly unchanged – and indeed they are on the outside.

Kirby Muxloe, Leicestershire	Closed in 1964, plans to reopen the station failed in the 1990s, yet in 2009 a second proposal was tabled.
Kirkbride, Cumbria	Closed in 1964, much of the area was demolished, although the station building survives as a private building.
Kirkby in Ashfield, Nottinghamshire	The present station is a new one; opening in 1990 it now handles some 170,000 passengers per annum. It replaced three stations: Kirkby in Ashfield Central, closed in 1962 and located to the west; Kirkby in Ashfield East, closed in 1965 and situated about 400yd away from the present station, half the distance from that which stood to the west; and Kirkby Bentick, closed in 1963 and positioned to the south-west in the village of Bentick.
Kirkintilloch, Glasgow	Closed in 1964.
Lakeside, Cumbria	Closed in 1965, it fell into disrepair until reopened in 1973 as part of the Lakeside & Haverthwaite Railway heritage line.
Lampeter, Gwynedd	Closed in 1965.
Lancaster Green Ayre, Lancashire	Closed in 1965, nothing of the old station remains.
Langford & Ulting, Essex	Closed in 1964.
Langley Mill, Derbyshire	Closed in 1963, it was demolished by 1976 when the trackbed became part of the Eastwood Bypass. Note that when it was closed it was in Nottinghamshire, but owing to boundary changes demolition took place in Derbyshire.
Larkhall, Lanarkshire	Closed in 1965, it reopened in 2005 and now handles more than 300,000 passengers annually a figure that is still growing.
Launceston, Cornwall	This was actually two stations standing back to back and serving two different lines. Both were operated from the same signal box, housing two independent frames. Officially known as Launceston North and Launceston South, these closed in 1964 and 1966 respectively. The site of both stations is now an industrial estate, with some parts being reused for the Launceston Steam Railway.
Launton, Oxfordshire	Closed in 1968.
Laurencekirk, Aberdeenshire	Closed in 1967 and reopening in 2009 at a cost of £3 million, more than 50,000 passengers come through the new station every day.
Leek, Staffordshire	Closed to passengers in 1965 and to freight five years later, the area is now the car park of a supermarket.
Leiston, Suffolk	Closed in 1966, a single line remained for staff training in 2005. Six years later, the possibility of running a service once more was investigated.

Levisham, North Yorkshire	Closed in 1965, it is now part of the North Yorkshire Moors Railway heritage line.
Lightcliffe, West Yorkshire	Closed in 1965.
Limpley Stoke, Wiltshire	Closed in 1965, the buildings are now privately owned.
Linton, Cambridgeshire	Closed in 1967.
Littleham, Devon	Closed in 1967, the stationmaster's house is now a private residence and the rest of the site is a housing estate.
Littleton & Badsey, Worcestershire	Closed in 1966.
Liverpool Road Halt, Staffordshire	Closed in 1964, the platforms were removed years ago but the trackbed now forms a pedestrian underpass.
Llandderfel, Gwynedd	Closed in 1964, all signs of the station have vanished.
Llandre, Ceredigion	Closed in 1965, this is another example of the arrival of the railways changing a place name: originally it was called Llanfihangel Genau'r Glyn, but when the railways decided to abbreviate this to just Llanfihangel, the local authorities asked them to change the name entirely as this represented one of the most common Welsh place names. The original name meant 'St Michael's at the mouth of the valley', while the modern name has no etymological value whatsoever.
Llandrillo, Denbighshire	Closed in 1964 due to flooding, a month before the scheduled closure.
Llanerchymedd, Anglesey	Closed in 1964, the site is owned by the Isle of Anglesey County Council and there are plans to develop it as a museum.
Llangefni, Anglesey	Closed in 1964, the sidings have been removed and now house a car park and the station buildings are privately owned; the line is still in place and there are talks to clear and reopen it to passenger services from Bangor.
Llangollen, Denbighshire	Closed in 1965, this now forms the terminus of the Llangollen heritage railway.
Llangower, Gwynedd	Closed in 1965, its reopening in 1972 (although not exactly on the original site) was to serve the Bala Lake Railway.
Llangwyllog, Anglesey	Closed in 1964, the track remains and the station buildings are privately owned.
Llangybi, Gwynedd	Closed in 1964.
Llanharan, Mid Glamorgan	Closed in 1964, a new station opened in 2007 following a campaign by local residents. Unmanned, with two platforms and a footbridge, the new station cost more than £4 million.
Llantwit Major, South Wales	Closed in 1965, the present station opened forty years later and now carries around 200,000 passengers annually.

Llanuwchllyn, Gwynedd	Closed in 1965, it reopened in 1972 as part of the Bala Light Railway. Of the original station, the cattle dock is now designated a picnic area, the goods shed a woodworking shop, and the building on platform two an office.
Llanwnda, Gwynedd	Closed in 1964, all signs of the station site have been eradicated by the traffic roundabout at the junction of two A roads.
Llys Halt, Gwynedd	Closed in 1965.
Loch Awe, Argyll & Bute	Closed in 1965, the station reopened in 1985.
Loch Tay, Stirling	Closed in 1965.
Lochwinnoch, Renfrewshire	Closed in 1966, little evidence remains of the station which is now covered by a housing development and the trackbed by National Cycle Network Route 7. However, since the station was situated on a bridge, access was via steps from underneath the bridge and that bricked-up entrance is quite evident.
Lodge Hill, Somerset	Closed in 1963, the site was soon cleared and some of the buildings reassembled elsewhere (such as Cranmore on the East Somerset Railway). As recently as 2002 the trackbed was used by light aircraft as a makeshift airfield.
Logierieve, Aberdeenshire	Closed in 1965.
Londesborough, East Yorkshire	Closed in 1965, the station building is now a private residence.
Long Melford, Suffolk	Closed in 1967, the station is now a private residence.
Longhope, Gloucestershire	Closed in 1964, all that remains is the waiting room building, now privately owned.
Low Moor, West Yorkshire	Closed in 1965, the site can just be made out among the vegetation alongside the line. It is planned to reopen a station here in 2013 as part of the Metro route.
Lubenham, Leicestershire	Closed in 1966.
Luffenham, Rutland	Closed in 1966.
Lugton, Ayrshire	Closed in 1966, the station buildings are still standing but were sold off with a planning application for development in the pipeline.
Luib, Stirling	Closed in 1965.
Luton Bute, Bedfordshire	Closed in 1965, the site was used as a car park until being extensively redeveloped as part of a guided busway scheme.
Luton Hoo, Bedfordshire	Closed in 1965, the station buildings and platform still exist but are unused.
Lydd-on-Sea Halt, Kent	Closed in 1967, the trackbed was lifted and the platform demolished; all that remains is a gated approach road.

Lydd Town, Kent	Closed in 1967, the buildings were used to repair cars until the 1980s; they are now derelict and the yard is used to store refuse collection wagons.
Lydford, Devon	Closed in 1964.
Lyme Regis, Dorset	Closed in 1965, the station building was dismantled brick by brick and reassembled at Alresford on the Watercress Line; the former site now houses a small industrial estate.
Lyng Halt, Somerset	Closed in 1964.
Maldon East & Heybridge, Essex	Closed in 1964.
Malvern Wells, Worcestershire	Closed in 1965, only the signal box remains.
Mangotsfield, Gloucestershire	Closed in 1966, parts of the station are still visible, especially from the Bristol and Bath Railway Path, National Cycle Network Route 4.
Manningham, West Yorkshire	Closed in 1965, the reopening of the station is still in the early planning stage.
Mansfield, Nottinghamshire	Closed in 1964, it reopened in 1995 and now handles some 400,000 passengers per annum.
Manton, Rutland	Closed in 1966, the station buildings now house a small industrial estate.
Marazion, Cornwall	Closed in 1969, one station building is now privately owned, but the remainder became derelict and were demolished.
Marfleet, Yorkshire	Closed in 1964.
Marishes Road, North Yorkshire	Closed in 1965, buildings have either been removed to other sites or demolished.
Market Weighton, Yorkshire	Closed in 1965, all the buildings were demolished in 1979.
Marsh Gibbon & Poundon, Buckinghamshire	Closed in 1968.
Maryhill, Glasgow	Closed in 1964, the station was demolished and the Maryhill Shopping Centre built in 1980; however, the basement area of the centre was left open to allow for the possible reopening of the line in the future. Any rumours of reopening were finally put to rest in 1999 when neighbouring land was sold to housing developers; the bridges crossing the line were demolished for safety reasons. When the shopping centre itself was demolished in 2010, the area beneath the new supermarket was again left empty, making it possible to reopen the line someday.
Masbury, Somerset	Closed in 1966, the site is now privately owned and crossed by a public footpath.

Mauchline, Ayrshire	Closed in 1965.
Maud Junction, Aberdeenshire	Closed in 1965, the station building is now home to the Maud Railway Station Museum, with a number of empty business units alongside. Remains of both the turntable and cattle-loading platforms can still be seen clearly.
Mayfield, Sussex	Closed in 1965, the station building is a private residence; the remaining buildings were cleared to make way for the bypass.
Meeth Halt, Devon	Closed in 1965, the short platform and stone shelter are still in use by walkers and cyclists using the trackbed now known as the Tarka Trail.
Meir, Staffordshire	Closed in 1966, nothing remains of the station today.
Melksham, Wiltshire	Closed in 1966, it reopened in 1985 and handled almost 40,000 passengers per annum, until a cut in the service to just two per weekday reduced this number to little more than 10,000.
Melton Constable, Norfolk	Closed in 1964, the station was demolished in 1971 and a telephone exchange built in its place.
Merchiston, Edinburgh	Closed in 1965, the station was quickly demolished and the trackbed made into a footpath.
Mickleton, North Yorkshire	Closed in 1964, the site is now a car park for walkers using the Tees Valley Railway Walk along the former trackbed.
Middleton, Greater Manchester	Closed in 1965.
Middleton-in-Teesdale, North Yorkshire	Closed in 1964.
Midford, Somerset	Closed in 1966, the trackbed has been surfaced as the cycleway known as the Two Tunnels Greenway. The station is owned by the new Somerset & Dorset Joint Railway, whose plans are discussed in Chapter 23.
Midsomer Norton, Somerset	Closed in 1966, the Somerset & Dorset Railway Heritage Trust own the site.
Milcote, Warwickshire	Closed in 1966, the trackbed was resurfaced by Sustrans as a path for walkers and cyclists.
Mill Hill, Isle of Wight	Closed in 1966, the topography still shows how the land was removed to allow entry to the tunnel, although nothing physical remains. When operational, virtually every passenger was going to or returning from work, hence the trains were full during rush hour but empty otherwise. Closure did not prevent one employee from doing the job he was paid to do: rather than risk a collision, for six months he manned the level crossing, although not a single train ran along the tracks and the level crossing gates never moved.

Midsomer Norton was a typical village railway station. (*Courtesy of Dr Ben Brooksbank*)

Miller's Dale, Derbyshire	Closed in 1967, the station buildings and platform are still here on what is now known as the Monsal Trail; the stationmaster's house and railway cottages are privately owned.
Millhouses, South Yorkshire	Closed in 1968, the buildings soon became derelict and remained so until the 1980s, when all but the stationmaster's house – now a private residence – were demolished. Reopening the station is debated regularly, although nothing has yet gone past the discussion stage.
Milliken Park, Renfrewshire	Closed in 1966, a new station opened to the south-west in 1989 and now handles some 150,000 passengers annually.
Mintlaw, Aberdeenshire	Closed in 1965.
Mitcheldean Road, Herefordshire	Closed in 1964, the site is now occupied by a housing estate.
Monton Green, Greater Manchester	Closed in 1969, some of the embankment remains and has been developed as a cycle path and walking route.
Morcott, Rutland	Closed in 1966.
Morebath Junction Halt, Devon	Closed in 1966 and now overgrown, it is still possible to discern something of the site. When operational, it proudly proclaimed itself to have the only signal box in Britain worked by a woman during the nineteenth century. Mrs Towns' employment lasted until at least 1913, by which time she had been there for twenty-three years.

Mountfield Halt, East Sussex	Closed in 1969, nothing of the site remains today.
Mow Cop & Scholar Green, Cheshire	Closed in 1964, all that remains is the signal box, now privately owned.
Muirkirk, Ayrshire	Closed in 1964.
Mumby Road, Lincolnshire	Closed in 1970.
Mundesley-on-Sea, Norfolk	Closed in 1964.
Muthill, Perth & Kinross	Closed in 1964, the site has been cleared and now boasts seven private homes and the offices of a business growing and exporting potatoes.
Nanstallon Halt, Cornwall	Closed in 1967.
Narborough, Leicestershire	Closed in 1968, public outcry reopened the station in 1970, when twenty-one months of disuse meant it was in need of restoration. Blaby Rural District and Blaby Parish Councils raised the £3,250 required to pay for the renovation.
Neen Sollars, Shropshire	Closed in 1964, the station building survives, although much of its original architecture has been reworked and it is not easily recognised.
Neilston, Renfrewshire	Closed in 1966, the trains still run along the line but all signs of the station are gone.
New Basford, Nottinghamshire	Closed in 1964, the stationmaster's house is still standing and privately owned; the rest of the site is now a housing estate.
Newchapel & Goldenhill, Staffordshire	Closed in 1964, the trackbed has been resurfaced as a footpath and while the station was demolished, something of the platform outline can still be discerned.
New Cumnock, Ayrshire	Closed in 1965, the station reopened in 1991 and now handles over 20,000 passengers annually.
New Romney & Littlestone-on-Sea, Kent	Closed in 1967, the trackbed can still be made out but nothing remains of the station site, which is now a small trading estate.
Newnham, Gloucestershire	Closed in 1964.
Newport, Isle of Wight	Closed in 1966 and demolished five years later, the trackbed is now a cycleway.
Newport, Shropshire	Closed in 1967, the possibility of reopening remains, with the growth of neighbouring Telford.
Newport Pagnall, Buckinghamshire	Closed in 1967, the site was redeveloped and is now home to a number of offices.
Newstead, Nottinghamshire	Closed in 1964, it reopened in 1993 and now handles in excess of 30,000 passengers per annum.

Newton Heath, Greater Manchester	Closed in 1966, the new Metrolink station is due to open in 2013.
Newton Poppleford, Devon	Closed in 1967, both the station and road bridge were demolished and nothing remains.
Normacot, Staffordshire	Closed in 1964, no sign of the station remains.
North Connel, Argyll & Bute	Closed in 1966, the station was demolished and all signs have been obliterated by the new trunk road constructed in 1990.
North Elmham, Norfolk	Closed in 1964, it is part of the planned additions of the Mid-Norfolk Railway, discussed in Chapter 7.
Northampton Bridge, Northamptonshire	Closed in 1964, the site remains but is now fenced off following an arson attack on the signal box.
Northenden, Greater Manchester	Closed in 1964, the site is still visible.
Nottingham Victoria, Nottinghamshire	Closed in 1967 and almost immediately demolished, all that remained was the station's impressive clock tower (256ft high). The clock was then incorporated into the Victoria Shopping Centre which still occupies the site.
Oakamoor, Staffordshire	Closed in 1965, the track remains and is owned by the Churnet Valley Railway who plan to run regular services along here eventually.
Oakley, Hampshire	Closed in 1963, the dilapidated station buildings still stand alongside the track.
Old Dalby, Leicestershire	Closed in 1968, the track was reused as the test track for the advanced passenger train and later for the Pendolino; the station building has disappeared but the goods shed remains.
Old Hill High Street, West Midlands	Closed in 1964.
Old Kilpatrick, Dumbartonshire	Closed in 1964, the platforms are still visible.
Oldland Common, Gloucestershire	Closed in 1966, the station is at the end of the Avon Valley Railway and on the Bristol and Bath Railway Path – both of which are covered in Chapter 6.
Otley, Yorkshire	Closed in 1965, a footpath for walkers follows the old trackbed through the cutting.
Otley & Ilkley, West Yorkshire	Closed in 1965, it reopened in 1974.
Ottery St Mary, Devon	Closed in 1967, the station building has been adopted by a youth club and the remainder of the site is now an industrial estate.
Ottringham, Yorkshire	Closed in 1964, the station is now a private house.

Oundle, Northamptonshire	Closed in 1964, the station is now a private residence. As discussed in Chapter 8, Nene Valley Railway hope to acquire much of the trackbed, but will never be able to come through to Oundle with the development now in place.
Oyne, Aberdeenshire	Closed in 1968.
Padbury, Buckinghamshire	Closed in 1964, the buildings were demolished four years later and there is now a small housing estate.
Padstow, Cornwall	Closed in 1967, the station building was initially used as the cycle hire shop for those walking and cycling the Camel Trail, which occupies the former trackbed.
Paisley, Renfrewshire	Closed in 1966, the site was demolished and is now a footpath.
Pampisford, Cambridgeshire	Closed in 1967.
Pans Lane Halt, Wiltshire	Closed in 1966, much of the station was demolished; what little did remain disappeared under the infill when the area became gardens.
Pant Glas, Gwynedd	Closed in 1965, the line is now a footpath, while the station's only building continues to offer shelter to those travelling along the route.
Parkhead Stadium, Glasgow	Closed in 1964.
Partick West, Glasgow	Closed in 1964.
Partington, Greater Manchester	Closed in 1964.
Partridge Green, West Sussex	Closed in 1966, the buildings were demolished and the area developed into a housing and industrial estate.
Paston & Knapton, Norfolk	Closed in 1964.
Patney & Chirton, Wiltshire	Closed in 1964, the station was demolished soon afterwards and today just the footbridge remains.
Patrington, Yorkshire	Closed in 1964.
Peak Forest, Derbyshire	Closed in 1967, the station buildings are now offices.
Peartree, Derbyshire	Closed in 1968, the line was reopened in 1976 for workers at Rolls-Royce. It remains open today but annual passenger numbers have not reached 3,000 for more than a decade.
Pelsall, West Midlands	Closed in 1965, the line remained open for almost twenty years.
Penally, Pembrokeshire	Closed in 1964, the station reopened just under eight years later and has seen regular use by around 5,000 passengers annually in the last forty years.

Penda's Way, West Yorkshire	Closed in 1964.
Penmaenpool, Gwynedd	Closed in 1965, the trackbed forms part of the Mawddach Trail. Note the station buildings have been absorbed by the George Hotel, while the former signal box was used as an observation post and information centre by the Royal Society for the Protection of Birds and the nature reserve.
Penns, West Midlands	Closed in 1965, the site is now an industrial estate.
Penton, Cumberland	Closed in 1969, the Waverley Route Heritage Association is at work to reopen part of the line.
Penwortham Cop Lane, Lancashire	Closed in 1964, local youths were quick to use the cutting for scrambling.
Penygroes, Gwynedd	Closed in 1964.
Peterhead, Aberdeenshire	Closed in 1965.
Petrockstow, Devon	Closed in 1965, it is now on the Tarka Trail.
Philorth, Aberdeenshire	Closed in 1965.
Pickering, North Yorkshire	Closed in 1965, the station was rebuilt as the southern terminus of the North Yorkshire Moors Railway, covered in Chapter 9.
Piershill, Edinburgh	Closed in 1964.
Pill, Somerset	Closed in 1964, discussions continue with a view to reopening the line.
Pinhoe, Devon	Closed in 1967, the station reopened in 1983. With passenger numbers now reaching 50,000 annually, and still increasing, its future seems assured.
Pipe Gate, Staffordshire	Closed in 1966, the station was demolished.
Pitcaple, Aberdeenshire	Closed in 1968.
Pitmedden, Aberdeenshire	Closed in 1964.
Pittenzie Halt, Perth & Kinross	Closed in 1964.
Pitts Hill, Staffordshire	Closed in 1964, little of the site remains.
Pocklington, Yorkshire	Closed in 1965, the station building is Grade II listed and doubles as the sports hall of Pocklington School.
Pont Rug Halt, Gwynedd	Closed in 1964, although it had been used for excursions only since 1932 when it ceased regular passenger services.
Pontrhythallt, Gwynedd	Closed in 1964, it too was used for excursions only since 1932.
Pool-in-Wharfedale, West Yorkshire	Closed in 1965.
Portishead, Somerset	Closed in 1964; the reopening of the line is in the planning stage, but will require the building of a new station because the original has been demolished.

Possil, Glasgow	Closed in 1964, the station building and yard still survive: the latter is now a scrapyard; the former, a bookmaker's from the 1980s, has been empty and derelict since 2006 but is protected as a Category C listed building.
Poyle Estate Halt, Buckinghamshire	Closed in 1965, no sign of its existence can be found today.
Poyle Halt, Surrey	Closed in 1965.
Puxton, Somerset	Closed in 1964, the stationmaster's house and platforms still exist; the goods shed was demolished around 2006 to make room for new houses.
Pyle, Bridgend	Closed in 1964, the present station handles over 50,000 passengers per annum and is situated about half a mile from the site of the original.
Pylle, Somerset	Closed in 1966.
Racks, Dumfries & Galloway	Closed in 1964, the station buildings are now private residences.
Radstock North, Somerset	Closed in 1966, the site has been landscaped as green space.
Ravenscar, North Yorkshire	Closed in 1964, the station is still visible; it is covered in Chapter 21 on the Cinder Track footpath.
Repton & Willington, Derbyshire	Closed in 1968, it reopened in the 1990s and now carries around 12,500 passengers annually.
Reston, Borders	Closed in 1964, proposals to reopen the station are currently being examined by the Scottish Parliament.
Rhoose, Vale of Glamorgan	Closed in 1965, the station reopened in 2005 as the Rhoose Cardiff International Airport Railway Station – the longest name for a railway station in the land which still appears on timetables.
Rhosgoch, Anglesey	Closed in 1964, the goods yard, sidings and station buildings are now owned by Anglesey County Council and a private investor.
Rhu, Argyll & Bute	The Beeching Axe closed the doors in 1964, which came as no surprise since the station had seen temporary and partial closures from 1941–50 and 1956–60.
Riccarton, Roxburghshire	Closed in 1969.
Ringstead & Addington, Northamptonshire	Closed in 1964, the approach is overgrown, but beneath the vegetation the sleeper blocks acting as stepping stones are still there.
Ringwood, Hampshire	Closed in 1964, the station site was demolished and is now an industrial estate; the former trackbed has been resurfaced as the Castleman Trailway, while a feasibility study in 2009 showed reopening the line was financially viable for an hourly service.
Roade, Northamptonshire	Closed in 1964, all traces of the station are long gone.

Robin Hood's Bay, North Yorkshire	Closed in 1965, the trackbed is now part of the Cinder Track path from Whitby to Scarborough, covered in Chapter 21.
Rocester, Staffordshire	Closed in 1965.
Rockingham, Leicestershire	Closed in 1966, the station does indeed lie in Leicestershire but was named after Rockingham in Northamptonshire. To confuse matters further, it was closest to Caldecott, which lies within the borders of the county of Rutland.
Romaldkirk, North Yorkshire	Closed in 1964.
Ross-on-Wye, Herefordshire	Closed in 1964, the goods and engine sheds stand in an area now redeveloped as an industrial estate.
Rotherfield & Mark Cross, East Sussex	Closed in 1965, the station building is now a private house.
Rowfant, West Sussex	Closed in 1967, much of the site is not only still there, but in use. The trackbed forms the public footpath known as the Worth Way, while the station and its goods yard are home to a road-building company.
Royston & Notton, South Yorkshire	Closed in 1968.
Royton, Greater Manchester	Closed in 1966.
Ruddington, Nottinghamshire	Closed in 1963, the buildings were demolished but the platform survives.
Rudgwick, West Sussex	Closed in 1965, the station was demolished soon afterwards; the trackbed is now part of the Downs Link footpath.
Rugeley, Staffordshire	Closed in 1965, the station reopened in 1997 and now handles over 100,000 passengers a year.
Rushcliffe Halt, Nottinghamshire	Closed in 1963, by the 1990s the line was preserved and services ran to Loughborough Junction. Eventual connection to the Great Central Railway heritage line is the obvious goal, but no timescale has been laid out.
Ruthwell, Dumfries & Galloway	Closed in 1965, the hamlet which grew up around the station took the name of Ruthwell Station, although historically it was known as Plans. No official name change can be traced so, once again, popular usage has prevailed.
Ryburgh, Norfolk	Closed in 1964, the station features in the plans of the Mid-Norfolk Railway heritage line and may form part of the Norfolk Orbital Railway scheme.
Saddleworth, Greater Manchester	Closed in 1968, the station is now a private residence.

Saffron Walden, Essex	Closed in 1964, the station is now a private residence and the yard a new housing development.
St Combs, Aberdeenshire	Closed in 1965.
Saltaire, West Yorkshire	Closed in 1965, the station reopened in 1984 and more than half a million passengers now pass through the gates every year.
Sampford Peverell, Devon	Closed in 1964, the site has been Tiverton Parkway Station since 1986 and now sees more than 350,000 passengers every year.
Sandwell & Banford, Somerset	Closed in 1963, it was preserved by a local company who used it as offices; it now forms part of a sheltered housing complex.
Sanquhar, Dumfries & Galloway	Closed in 1965, the station reopened in 1994 and now handles some 25,000 passengers every year.
Scorrier, Cornwall	Closed in 1964.
Scotswood, Northumberland	Closed in 1967.
Sealand, Flintshire	Closed in 1968, the trackbed has been resurfaced as a cycleway.
Seaton, Rutland	Closed in 1966, the site is now a scrapyard.
Seaton Junction, Devon	Closed in 1966, the station building is now a private residence; the platform remains but is overgrown, while the most obvious relic is the footbridge.
Seend, Wiltshire	Closed in 1966, the site was demolished in 1970.
Semington Halt, Wiltshire	Closed in 1966, the station is now a private residence.
Semley, Wiltshire	Closed in 1966, the site is now shared by an industrial estate and commercial centre.
Severn Bridge, Gloucestershire	Closed in 1964, the site quickly became derelict.
Shandon, Argyll & Bute	Closed in 1964, the signal box was removed in 1967 and with the exception of the loading bank, nothing of the station remains.
Shap, Cumbria	Closed in 1968.
Shapwick, Somerset	Closed in 1966, the site was cleared.
Sharpness, Gloucestershire	Closed in 1964.
Sheepbridge, Derbyshire	Closed in 1967, the booking office was home to a television repair shop.
Shepton Mallet Charlton Road, Somerset	Closed in 1966.
Sherburn-in-Elmet, North Yorkshire	Closed in 1965 but reopened in 1984, it now handles more than 20,000 passengers every year.
Shields Road, Glasgow	Closed in 1966.

Shillingstone, Somerset	Closed in 1966, railway enthusiasts have been working for more than a decade to reopen the station as an attraction.
Shoscombe & Single Hill Halt, Somerset	Closed in 1966; by 1968 the site was overgrown and hardly recognisable.
Shrivenham, Oxfordshire	Closed in 1964; demolition the following year removed the buildings but left something of the platforms.
Sidley, East Sussex	Closed in 1964, the buildings were demolished at various times; the goods shed was the last to go in 2009.
Sidmouth, Devon	Closed in 1967, the station buildings are now offices.
Sidmouth Junction, Devon	Closed in 1965, the buildings were demolished soon after; the station reopened in 1971 as Feniton and a new ticket office was built three years later. There were further improvements to the station in 1992.
Sigglesthorne, Yorkshire	Closed in 1964, the station is now a private residence.
Sileby, Leicestershire	Closed in 1968 and reopened in 1994, the station house is all that remains of the original station, which now sees more than 100,000 passengers annually.
Silloth, Cumbria	Closed in 1964, the site was cleared in 2006 and single-parent housing built in its place.
Silverdale, Staffordshire	Closed in 1964, the platforms have been repaired recently as part of a railway footpath.
Skelmanthorpe, West Yorkshire	Closed in 1983, it reopened nine years later.
Skewen, Neath Port Talbot	Closed in 1964, the station reopened thirty years later and now handles 30,000 passengers each year.
Skipton, Yorkshire	Closed in 1965.
Slaithwaite, West Yorkshire	Closed in 1968, it reopened in 1982 and sees nearly 200,000 passengers a year.
Slinfold, West Sussex	Closed in 1965, two railway cottages remain while the rest of the station area is now a caravan park.
Southam Road & Harbury, Warwickshire	Closed in 1964, the station was demolished and little evidence remains.
Southcoates, Yorkshire	Closed in 1964, the station was demolished soon after.
Southwater, West Sussex	Closed in 1966, the track is now part of the Downs Way footpath and the station site holds Horsham District Council offices.
Spon Lane, West Midlands	Closed in 1964, little evidence of a station remains today.
Springside, Ayrshire	Closed in 1964, little remains of the station today.
Stacksteads, Lancashire	Closed in 1966.
Staines West, Surrey	Closed in 1965, the station was demolished and the station building is now used as offices.

Staintondale, North Yorkshire	Closed in 1965, the station building is now a private residence.
Stalbridge, Dorset	Closed in 1966, today the area is a trading estate.
Stamford Bridge, Yorkshire	Closed in 1965, the station has been taken over as a private members' club for the village.
Stanley Bridge Halt, Wiltshire	Closed in 1965.
Staple Hill, Gloucestershire	Closed in 1966, the trackbed is now a cycle path from which some of the platforms can still be seen.
Steeton & Silsden, Yorkshire	Closed in 1965 and reopened in 1990, the original station building is now a private residence; the new station sees 650,000 passengers per annum.
Stepney, East Yorkshire	Closed in 1964, the station building has been awarded a Grade II listing.
Steventon, Oxfordshire	Closed in 1964, the site was demolished soon afterwards.
Stewarton, Ayrshire	Closed in November 1966, the station reopened just nine months later. In 1975 the service was reduced to a single track and one platform, only to be returned to a double track and two platforms in 2009 to accommodate 200,000 passengers annually.
Steyning, West Sussex	Closed in 1966, the trackbed forms part of the Downs Link footpath, while the old warehouse building has been converted into living accommodation.
Stockport Tiviot, Lancashire	Closed in 1967, the site is now shared between a supermarket and offices.
Stoke, Suffolk	Closed in 1967.
Stoke Works, Worcestershire	Closed in 1966.
Stonehouse (Bristol Road), Gloucestershire	Closed in 1965.
Stow, Borders	Closed in 1969, reopening is planned for 2014.
Stranraer, Wigtownshire	Closed in 1966.
Strata Florida, Ceredigion	Closed in 1965.
Strathyre, Stirling	Closed in 1965.
Streetly, West Midlands	Closed in 1965, the buildings were demolished soon afterwards.
Strichen, Aberdeenshire	Closed in 1965.
Sturmer, Essex	Closed in 1967.
Sturminster Newton, Dorset	Closed in 1966, it is now a trading estate, with commemorative gates informing us this was once part of the Somerset & Dorset Joint Railway.
Stutton, North Yorkshire	Closed in 1966.

Sutton-on-Hull, Yorkshire	Closed in 1964, everything but the stationmaster's house – now a private residence – was soon demolished.
Sutton Park, West Midlands	Closed in 1965.
Swanbourne, Buckinghamshire	Closed in 1968, the site is now completely overgrown.
Swine, Yorkshire	Closed in 1964.
Symington, Lanarkshire	Closed in 1965, little of the station remains.
Syston, Leicestershire	Closed in 1968, the area was fenced off until 2006 when the station building was removed and rebuilt at Butterley; a new housing estate was built on the Syston site.
Tadcaster, North Yorkshire	Closed in 1966, the station building is all that remains and is a private residence.
Talacre, Denbighshire	Closed in 1966, one platform and the sidings still survive, a result of serving a nearby mine until 1996. The mine site was soon cleared but some of the station remains.
Tavistock, Devon	Closed in 1968, the station now houses luxury apartments and is discussed in Chapter 30.
Tebay, Cumbria	Closed in 1968, the station and buildings were demolished and no trace remains.
Templecombe, Somerset	Closed in 1968, the station buildings were demolished two years later. After a number of trials the new station opened in 1983 and now sees 200,000 passengers a year.
Theddingworth, Leicestershire	Closed in 1966, the buildings are kept in excellent condition by the new owners.
Thornhill, Dumfries & Galloway	Closed in 1965, some of the station buildings are still visible. Unusually, plans to reopen the station in 2009 were vehemently opposed by residents who claimed the new buildings would severely affect their quality of life.
Thorpe, Northamptonshire	Closed in 1964.
Thorpeness, Suffolk	Closed in 1966, the platforms are all that survive; they are overgrown but visible from the trackbed which is not a footpath.
Thrapston Bridge Street, Northamptonshire	Closed in 1964.
Tipton St Johns, Devon	Closed in 1967, the station building and its platform now comprise a private residence.
Tiverton, Devon	Closed in 1964, the station was later demolished and covered by the relief road system.
Todd Lane Junction, Lancashire	Closed in 1968, the trackbed is now a footpath and cycleway.
Tollcross, Glasgow	Closed in 1964.

Torrington, Devon	Closed in 1965, occasional specials and freight still ran until 1982; the station was converted into a public house.
Trent, Derbyshire	Closed in 1968, the buildings were demolished shortly afterwards.
Trevor, Denbighshire	Closed in 1965.
Trouble House Halt, Gloucestershire	Closed in 1964, this was claimed to be the only railway stop in the country to serve a public house. In the earliest days the landlord provided a crate at each door to allow travellers to board or disembark. As the last trains travelled these tracks, burning hay bales blocked the route and suitably dressed mourners loaded a coffin on to the train. The coffin was filled with empty whisky bottles and sent via Kemble to Paddington, although it may not have reached its intended recipient, Dr Beeching himself.
Tullibardine, Perth & Kinross	Closed in 1964.
Tunstall, Staffordshire	Closed in 1964, the site was demolished except for the stationmaster's house, now a private residence; the trackbed has become part of the Potteries Greenway.
Tweedmouth, Northumberland	Closed in 1964, the line is still open and the platforms are *in situ*.
Tyldesley, Lancashire	Closed in 1969, the trackbed is now a footpath. For some time the station has been suggested as a good candidate for a guided bus route.
Udny, Aberdeenshire	Closed in 1965.
Uffington, Oxfordshire	Closed in 1964, the station buildings were demolished soon afterwards.
Uplawmoor, Renfrewshire	Closed in 1966, the station building is now a private residence.
Ushaw Moor, County Durham	Closed in 1964, the buildings were demolished and the trackbed has become part of the Deerness Valley Railway Path.
Valley, Anglesey	Closed in 1966, it reopened sixteen years later almost to the day and now handles around 16,000 passengers annually.
Ventnor, Isle of Wight	Closed in 1966, the station was demolished shortly afterwards.
Verney Junction, Buckinghamshire	Closed in 1968, the stationmaster's house is now a private residence.
Verwood, Dorset	Closed in 1964, an embankment and a couple of bridges are the only signs of a former railway.
Vulcan Halt, Greater Manchester	Closed in 1965, it has now been developed and more than 600 homes occupy the foundry site.

Wadebridge, Cornwall	Closed in 1965, the station building is now the Betjeman Centre, the goods shed a youth club, and the trackbed a road leading to a housing estate built around the site of the former engine shed. Plans to reopen the line and station are currently in the earliest stages.
Wakerley & Barrowden, Northamptonshire	Closed in 1966.
Walsingham, Norfolk	Closed in 1964, three years later the station buildings were acquired by members of the Russian Orthodox Church and converted for use as a small monastic community.
Wantage Road, Oxfordshire	Closed in 1964, the buildings were demolished shortly afterwards, but the platforms are still visible.
Warmley, Gloucestershire	Closed in 1966, the trackbed has become the Bristol and Bath Railway Path and the platform shelter a refreshment stop.
Waterfoot, Lancashire	Closed in 1966.
Watergate Halt, Devon	Closed in 1966, it is now part of the Tarka Trail footpath and cycle route.
Waterhouses, County Durham	Closed in 1964, the demolished station site is now a park and the trackbed forms part of the Deerness Valley Railway Path.
Wath North, South Yorkshire	Closed in 1968, subsidence caused the eventual closure of the line in 1986, by which time little of the station was still standing.
Watton, Norfolk	Closed in 1964.
Wednesbury, West Midlands	Closed in 1964, the buildings were demolished shortly afterwards, but the platform remains today.
Welford & Kilworth, Leicestershire	Closed in 1966, the buildings were demolished soon afterwards, except for the down platform shelter which was preserved at the Coventry Railway Centre.
Wellingborough London Road, Northamptonshire	Closed in 1966, all signs of the station have gone, although the line of the trackbed can be seen.
Wellington, Somerset	Closed in 1964, the goods shed is still standing but derelict.
Wellow, Somerset	Closed in 1966, the station building and signal box were converted into residential properties.
Wells Tucker Street, Somerset	Closed in 1963, the station was demolished; the railway cottages, however, are still homes and the goods shed is used for commercial purposes.
Wells-next-the-Sea, Norfolk	Closed in 1964, the station building was occupied by a second-hand bookshop and the corn mill was converted into flats; the site is now an industrial estate.
West Grinstead, West Sussex	Closed in 1966, the station and trackbed are still in use as part of the Downs Link footpath.

West Hallam, Derbyshire	Closed in 1964, the station building is now a private residence and the base of the garden centre.
West Moors, Dorset	Closed in 1964.
West Pennard, Somerset	Closed in 1966, the station building is now a private residence.
West Timperley, Greater Manchester	Closed in 1964.
Weston under Penyard Halt, Worcestershire	Closed in 1964, nothing of the station remains.
Wetheral, Cumbria	Closed in 1967, the station reopened in 1981 and, while unstaffed, now handles over 10,000 passengers per annum.
Wetherby Linton Road, West Yorkshire	Closed in 1964, nothing remains except for the platform edge and something of the foundations.
Weybourne, Norfolk	Closed in 1964, it reopened in 1975 as part of the Mid-Norfolk Railway, a line discussed in Chapter 7.
Wheathampstead, Hertfordshire	Closed in 1965, the track was lifted and the station became overgrown; in 2010 volunteers cleared the site, introduced new station signs, and a bench was installed to commemorate the 150th anniversary of the original opening of the station.
Whitedale, Yorkshire	Closed in 1964, the station building is now a private residence.
Whiteinch, Glasgow	Closed in 1964.
Whitwell, Derbyshire	Closed in 1964, the station building was dismantled and rebuilt at Butterley in 1981. Whitwell was reopened in 1998 and now handles more than 20,000 passengers annually.
Wickham Bishops, Essex	Closed in 1964.
Wickwar, Gloucestershire	Closed in 1965, the buildings were demolished with the exception of the stationmaster's house, which is now a private residence.
Wigan, Lancashire	Closed in 1964, the site was redeveloped forty years later as the Grand Arcade Shopping Centre.
Wighton Halt, Norfolk	Closed in 1964, the station reopened in 1984 as part of the Wells & Walsingham Light Railway.
Willenhall Bilston Street, West Midlands	Closed in 1965, plans to reopen the station have been shelved.
Wilmington, Yorkshire	Closed in 1964, only the booking office still stands.
Wilton South, Wiltshire	Closed in 1966, little evidence of the station remains.
Wimblington, Cambridgeshire	Closed in 1967, the site was cleared in 1971 and is now buried beneath the bypass.
Wimborne, Dorset	Closed in 1964, demolition followed and it is now the site of Wimborne's popular weekly market.

Wincanton, Somerset	Closed in 1966.
Windmill End, West Midlands	Closed in 1964; the site was demolished fifty years later, so it is almost impossible to see where the buildings once were as the vegetation has closed in.
Wingfield, Derbyshire	Closed in 1967, the buildings remain.
Winscombe, Somerset	Closed in 1963, the platform and seating have been reinstated as part of the Cheddar Valley Railway Walk.
Witham, Somerset	Closed in 1966, little evidence of the station remains today.
Withernsea, Yorkshire	Closed in 1964.
Withyham, East Sussex	Closed in 1967, the station building is now a private residence, fittingly called Other Withyham Station. The trackbed forms part of the Worth Way and Forest Way footpaths and cycle routes.
Wnion Halt, Gwynedd	Closed in 1965.
Woodford Halse, Northamptonshire	Closed in 1966, the site was later used to display touring caravans for sale.
Wookey, Somerset	Closed in 1963, the wooden buildings were cleared soon afterwards.
Wootton Bassett, Wiltshire	Closed in 1965, the siding is still in use to bring limestone quarried in the Mendip Hills to the distribution depot.
Worsley, Greater Manchester	Closed in 1969, nothing of the station remains.
Wroxall, Isle of Wight	Closed in 1966, the down part of the station was demolished, while the Station Hotel on the up platform was converted into housing.
Yarde Halt, Devon	Closed in 1965, it now forms part of the Tarka Trail.
Yate, Gloucestershire	Closed in 1965, it reopened in 1989 and now sees more than a quarter of a million passengers annually.
Yelvertoft & Stanford Park, Northamptonshire	Closed in 1966.
Yeovil, Somerset	Closed in 1967, the site was demolished and became a car and coach park for many years; in recent years a cinema and leisure centre have been constructed here.
Ynys, Gwynedd	Closed in 1964.

32 THE MEDIA

Research has revealed a number of items which, while they could never be considered a direct result of the Beeching Axe, could not have existed without the cuts being made. The sheer diversity of these offerings means it is impossible to fit them under other headings; therefore, they must be included in this section.

The year of the report saw headlines splashed across every newspaper. One reader, reputedly scanning a list of proposed closures in *The Guardian*, took up his pen and began to write a lyric. That man was Michael Flanders who, together with his colleague Donald Swann, penned the song the *Slow Train*. Flanders and Swann produced around 100 satirical comedy songs in a recording career lasting from 1956 to 1967. There are some inaccuracies in the lyrics, although this has been said to be the result of the station names being reproduced erroneously in the original newspaper article. However, it could be simply due to the lyric not scanning properly.

The song has other versions: electronica duo Lemon Jelly used samples from The King's Singers recording of 1976 in their version; while 2004 saw the release of a themed album by the Canadian classical quartet Quartetto Gelato, who used a slightly different version to introduce their travels on the Orient Express in words and music. Flanders and Swann have recently been lampooned by comedy duo Armstrong and Miller, the former seated in a wheelchair with a blanket over his legs and the latter seated at the piano. The original duo were also seated during every performance – the bespectacled Swann to play the piano and the bearded Flanders in a wheelchair as a result of contracting poliomyelitis in 1943.

Flanders and Swann considered their song to be rather different for them, for the subject matter, although treated with some mirth, was a serious one, especially in those dark days of 1963 when Richard Beeching was rarely out of the headlines. Nevertheless, for those who remember that year, the lyric is still a poignant one:

Miller's Dale for Tideswell, Kirby Muxloe, Mow Cop and Scholar Green.
No more will I go to Blandford Forum and Mortenhoe
On the slow train from Midsomer Norton and Mumby Road
No churns, no porter, no cat on a seat
At Chorlton-cum-Hardy or Chester-le-Street
We won't be meeting again
On the Slow Train
I'll travel no more from Littleton Badsey to Openshaw
At Long Stanton I'll stand well clear of the doors no more
No whitewashed pebbles, no up and no down

From Formby Four Crosses to Dunstable Town
I won't be going again
On the Slow Train
On the main line and the goods siding
The grass grows high
At Dog Dyke, Tumby Woodside
And Trouble House Halt
The sleepers sleep at Audlem and Ambergate
No passenger waits on Chittening platform or Cheslyn Hay
No one departs, no one arrives
From Selby to Goole, from St Erth to St Ives
They've all passed out of our lives
On the Slow Train, on the Slow Train
Cockermouth for Buttermere, on the Slow Train, Armley Moor Arram, Pye
Hill and Somercotes, on the Slow Train, Windmill End …

There is another song about Beeching himself entitled *The Beeching Report*. Recorded by iLiKETRAiNS, the lyrics are reinforced by the accompanying video, which features a group of insects coming together to form a human shape, preparing to take on Dr Beeching. Beeching, however, is unafraid and sweeps the insects aside to crush them. The insects represent those who lost their jobs as a result of the accursed report.

Comedy scriptwriter Laurie Wyman was not slow to weave the news of the day into his stories. An episode of *The Navy Lark*, broadcast on BBC radio in October 1963, included Able Seaman Goldstein reporting back late to Portsmouth and HMS *Troutbridge* owing to his local railway station being closed. At the time, the railways were in the news for other reasons, too. This episode also regularly suggested Chief Petty Officer Pertwee, a character renowned more for his black market dealings than for his role as a navy man, was rumoured to be absent because of a certain train robbery in August of that year.

Years after the report, Richard Beeching got his own television series at the BBC. Well, almost. Broadcast for two series in the mid-1990s and filmed on the Severn Valley Railway, *Oh, Doctor Beeching!* was created by David Croft and Richard Spendlove. The cast were largely drawn from two other BBC sitcom staples of the day: *Hi-de-Hi!* and *Are You Being Served?* The series, however, never came near the success of the others, probably because it first hit the television schedules over thirty years after the report.

The title reflected the comedy film classic *Oh, Mr Porter!* starring Will Hay. Indeed, the series' theme tune, sung by Su Pollard, uses the same tune but changes the words to suit this scenario:

Oh, Dr Beeching, what have you done?
There once were lots of trains to catch, but soon there will be none,
I'll have to buy a bike, 'cos I can't afford a car,
Oh, Dr Beeching, what a naughty man you are!

33   IN CONCLUSION

Fifty years have now passed since the publication of the dreaded document and yet feelings hardly seem to have changed towards Richard Beeching. With the benefit of hindsight, perhaps the time is right to take a fresh look at the situation, both in 1963 and in the ensuing five decades.

Even at the time it was generally accepted that something had to be done to change the dreadfully inefficient railway system then operating in Britain. Two things raised the hackles of the public at the very mention of Richard Beeching's name: first, he had no experience or background in railways; and second, his annual salary was plastered all over the front of the *Daily Mirror*, revealing he was earning more than twice as much as the prime minister. Together, these made him public enemy number one virtually overnight.

While his record shows he was certainly qualified to do the job, undoubtedly Beeching made mistakes. During this author's research, interviews with numerous individuals, all much better qualified and knowledgeable than the author, repeatedly revealed the same complaint: the many closures served only to fragment adjoining services. For example, when a passenger's commute required two trains in each direction and one of those journeys underwent closures to some degree, that passenger had to seek an alternative route away from the railways; closing one line and/or station took the passenger off the second line. Commuters who took two trains to and from work were the exception, but the same applied to other journeys.

The most common solution was a replacement bus service. Buses are cheaper to run and better suited to transporting fewer passengers. A bus also shares the road with many other vehicles and is thus prone to delays, much more than a train service – only trains run on tracks. It is also true that trains are seen as more desirable than buses for a multitude of reasons – faster, reliable and more comfortable. Even freedom of movement may be seen as a factor; neither refreshments nor a toilet will be available on a bus. Records show where a replacement bus service was made available, it was shunned. Further research proves the commuters either changed their jobs or purchased a car.

It should be noted that Richard Beeching did not set his own salary when the five-year contract was offered. As stated in Chapter 2, the offer was made in order to tempt him away from his position at ICI; even on the temporary basis, remuneration had to be more than he was currently earning at the chemicals giant. Hence, he can hardly be held responsible for his salary; perhaps he should be lauded for ending his five-year contract at the end of four years, effectively turning down £24,000.

Richard Beeching was also extremely unlucky. Factors he had neither control over nor could have envisaged as having such an influence crept up on him. Only one could he have had any influence over. The old wooden vans had carried goods all over the land, had loaded and unloaded at stations, passing through junctions and marshalling yards, joining and leaving trains to reach their destination for decades. A simple procedure but one which was extraordinarily inefficient and labour intensive and could be handed over to road traffic. The wooden vans were disposed of and more efficient freight was seen as the answer. With new hopper-loading for ores and coal, vast tonnages could be moved quickly and cheaply across the country. Investing in lines to bring coal to local power stations was seen as guaranteed work, for lorries could never move the tonnage required. While the assumption was sound enough, the reduction in the number of power plants and the increase in pylons and the national grid meant the power stations were nearer the coal. There was no longer any requirement for moving massive amounts of mined minerals.

The car was still a luxury item. However, this rapidly changed in the early 1960s. Not only did the average family have the means to purchase their own car, but manufacturers started producing affordable models. These cars also found fast, open roads opening up to them. The introduction of the motorway meant car travel could challenge train travel in journey times, with the added advantage of a direct route. Very quickly, lines retained for freight were closed through lack of demand. Replacement buses became uneconomical and went the same way as the trains. Yet off the rails the situation was looking rosy. Car manufacturers were enjoying a boom period, as were the road builders, for thousands more cars appeared on the roads.

Britain's first motorway, officially known as the Preston Bypass but effectively the M6, opened in December 1958. By the time of the release of the Reshaping of Britain's Railways report, nearly 200 miles of motorway had been opened. Over the next ten years another 1,000 miles of motorway were made available to the public with their cars and to businesses, with increasing numbers of lorries emerging with seemingly ever-larger carrying capacities.

There is one connection between Richard Beeching, the report of 1963, and the unstoppable ribbons of motorways spreading out across the mainland of Britain. That connection is Ernest Marples. In 1957 Marples became postmaster general in the cabinet of Prime Minister Harold Macmillan. In this position he introduced Subscriber Trunk Dialling for telephone users (prior to this, national calls had to be connected via the operator), he began the new Premium Bond scheme, and oversaw the introduction of the country's first postcodes.

By 1959 Marples had been appointed Minister of Transport. In this role he brought in the provisional licence for learner drivers, the annual MOT test for cars, parking meters, yellow lines and traffic wardens to prevent us parking our newly MOT'd cars. Such unpopular decisions are largely forgotten in the light of what was to follow: the report on the railways.

Ernest Marples had a number of business interests prior to his political career. Since the late 1940s he had been a director of Kirk & Kirk. It was in this capacity that he first met civil engineer Reginald Ridgway, and in 1948 the pair founded Marples, Ridgway & Partners – a civil engineering company which soon grew large enough to take over Kirk & Kirk. The new company acquired several contracts for building new power stations in England and hydroelectric stations in Scotland, roads in both Ethiopia and England, and a new port in Jamaica.

Note how these new power stations and roads are also connected with Ernest Marples. When his political career began to blossom he did resign his directorship but retained his shares. When the Attorney General pointed out a conflict of interests should he continue to be the majority shareholder in the company, Marples attempted to sell his shares to Ridgway. However, this was blocked as it was clear he intended to use Ridgway as an agent and buy back his shares as soon as he could. When this plan was scuppered he sold the shares to his wife, thus enabling him to buy back those shares at the original price when he left political office.

As the newly appointed Minister of Transport, Marples opened the first section of the M1 motorway in 1959. While a direct link between Marples Ridgway and the M1 has never been revealed, undoubtedly the two men had their proverbial finger in this profitable pie. This was also the case with the subsequent construction of the Hammersmith Flyover, Chiswick Flyover, and the later extension of the M1 into London.

When Marples left office in 1964, with the Conservatives having lost the election to a Harold Wilson-led Labour party, his small investment from the late 1940s had mushroomed into shares worth at least £350,000. To put this into perspective, it is equal in spending power to at least eight times this amount today – and that figure of £350,000 is the absolute minimum value; in reality it was probably much more.

No stranger to controversy and scandal, Marples was investigated in 1963 by Lord Denning when Denning was producing his report on the so-called Profumo Affair. While there was never any suggestion Marples was involved in the scandal, it does seem Denning reported to Harold Macmillan that his

Minister of Transport was in the habit of entertaining himself with a succession of prostitutes – doubtless he could afford them – although these facts did not appear in the final report.

Despite being out of government, the former minister continued to represent his constituents in the House of Commons until 1974 when he retired from politics. It was in the following year that the public were finally made aware of Marples' personal and business life. When news of his tax evasion broke, it transpired he had fled the country, having moved most of his assets out of Britain through a company he had set up in Liechtenstein. While the Treasury attempted to freeze his assets, it was already too late. Leaving his clothing and possessions littering the floor of his Belgravia home, he sailed for France on the night ferry.

In a later interview he claimed he fled when confronted by a demand to pay the tax he had avoided for the last thirty years. Ernest Marples never returned to British shores; he lived in Monaco and France until his death in July 1978.

With regard to Britain's railways, it seems Marples, as the man who gave Beeching the job of looking at the required cuts, was more concerned with personal profit than the good of either the railways or the nation. Indeed, Dr Beeching probably had more reason to despise his employer than anyone.

Richard Beeching certainly made mistakes, yet fifty years on it seems he was not the demonic figure in the Reshaping of the Railways. It is probably true to say that Beeching's single biggest mistake was taking the job in the first place. He was in a no-win situation almost as soon as he signed the contract and this would have been true of whoever took on the task. While Richard Beeching's name will forever be linked to the decimation of the railway system, and he will forever be 'the axeman', he was only a puppet figure. The real demon behind the report was the Minister of Transport – Alfred Ernest Marples.

OTHER TITLES PUBLISHED BY THE HISTORY PRESS

Signal Box Coming Up, Sir!

Geoff Body and Bill Parker

978-0-7524-6040-6

There's never a dull moment in this entertaining collection of experiences as Geoff Body and Bill Parker present often hilarious highlights from the careers of railwaymen around Britain over the last fifty years.

Along Different Lines

Geoff Body and Bill Parker

978-0-7524-8915-5

Running a railway is a complex business. However well run it is there will always be surprises, often hilarious, frequently unexpected, sometimes serious. Here railway professionals recall notable incidents from across their careers on the railways, in this second collection lovingly compiled by Geoff Body and Bill Parker.

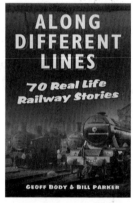

Saving the West Somerset Railway

John Parsons

978-0-7524-6403-9

The West Somerset Railway opened in 1862, linking Taunton, Watchet and Minehead, but was closed by British Rail in 1971. This book tells the story of the small group of enthusiasts, many of whom still work on the railway today, who refused to let the line die.

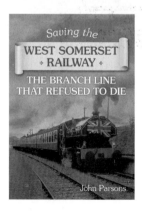

Visit our website and discover thousands of other History Press books.
www.thehistorypress.co.uk